D1223369

COLONIAL

New Jersey

John T. Cunningham

Thomas Nelson Inc.
New York   Camden

HILLSBOROUGH TWP. PUBLIC
LIBRARY ASSOCIATION

SOMERSET COUNTY LIBRARY
SOMERVILLE, N. J.

Photographs are from the following sources: Author's collection, pp. 33, 43, 60, 70, 111, 113, 127, 135, 143; Newark Sunday News, pp. 6, 117; Library of Congress, pp. 10, 18, 121; Newark Public Library, pp. 12, 50, 72, 97, 100, 107; New Jersey State Museum, pp. 14, 15, 27; New Jersey Department of Environmental Protection, pp. 17, 109, 112, 135; New York Historical Society, pp. 21, 49, 122; American-Swedish Historical Museum, p. 22; New Jersey Tercentenary Commission, p. 30; Irving Tuttle, pp. 31, 72, 74, 149; Frutchey Associates, p. 36; Mrs. M. L. Budd, p. 39; Louis Checkman, p. 52; Salem County Historical Society, p. 61; Dr. Henry S. Bisbee, p. 64; Alex Sibirny, p. 28; Atkinson's *History of Newark*, pp. 116, 118; New Jersey Historical Society, pp. 54–55, 121, 129; New Jersey State Library, p. 130; Trenton State College, p. 131; William F. Cone, pp. 3, 44, 139; Dahlmeyer Studios, p. 146; Ellis and Snyder's *A Brief History of New Jersey*, pp. 87, 140.

Copyright 1971 by John T. Cunningham

All rights reserved under International and Pan-American Conventions. Published in Camden, New Jersey, by Thomas Nelson & Sons and simultaneously in Toronto, Canada, by Thomas Nelson & Sons (Canada) Limited.

Library of Congress Catalog Card Number: 73–145920
ISBN: 0-8407-7110-X (trade); ISBN: 08407-7111-8 (library)

Printed in the United States of America

2

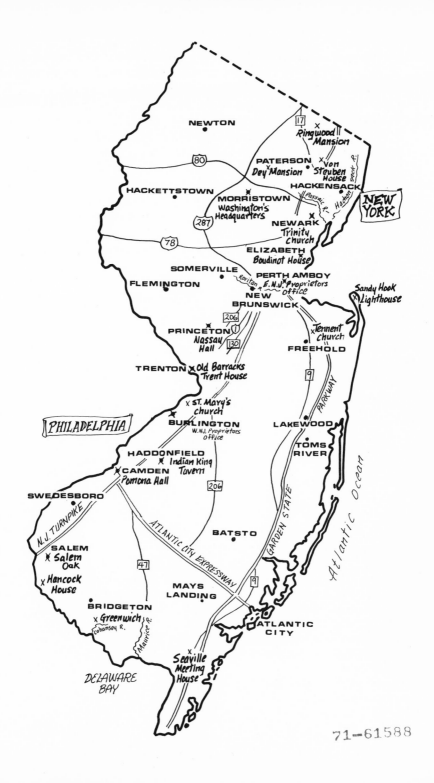

NEWTON

Ringwood Mansion ×

17

PATERSON
Dey Mansion
von
Steuben
House

80

HACKETTSTOWN

HACKENSACK

MORRISTOWN
Washington's
Headquarters

NEW
YORK

287

NEWARK
Trinity
Church

78

ELIZABETH
× Boudinot House

SOMERVILLE

PERTH AMBOY
× E.N.J. Proprietors
Office

FLEMINGTON

Raritan R.

NEW
BRUNSWICK

Sandy Hook
× Lighthouse

206

PRINCETON
Nassau
Hall

130

Tennent
× Church

FREEHOLD

TRENTON × Old Barracks
Trent House

9

PARKWAY

× St. Mary's
church

PHILADELPHIA

BURLINGTON
W.N.J. Proprietors
Office

LAKEWOOD

HADDONFIELD
× Indian King
Tavern

TOMS
RIVER

CAMDEN ×
Pomona Hall

206

Atlantic Ocean

SWEDESBORO

N.J. TURNPIKE

ATLANTIC CITY EXPRESSWAY

BATSTO

GARDEN STATE

SALEM
× Salem
Oak

47

× Hancock
House

MAYS
LANDING

9

BRIDGETON
× Greenwich
Cohansey R.

Maurice R.

ATLANTIC
CITY

DELAWARE
BAY

× Seaville
Meeting
House

71—61588

Contents

In West New Jersey, the Quakers built their towns around their meeting-houses. Most of them were quite large, two stories in height and built of red brick, such as this meetinghouse in Crosswicks close by a giant oak tree.

6

Prologue

Nature made certain that the long peninsula now called New Jersey would occupy a central role in the development of an emerging nation called America. The peninsula pushes against the Atlantic Ocean about midway between Nova Scotia and Florida. Natural sea currents and prevailing winds swept early explorers along the coast, ensuring that some of them would sail by and perhaps stop for a look—as did Giovanni da Verrazano in 1524 and Henry Hudson in 1609.

Leading inward from the rolling Atlantic were the two deep mouths of the rivers that we now call Hudson and Delaware, natural thoroughfares to the interior. Henry Hudson and Samuel Argall each explored one of the rivers, the former in Holland's name and the latter for England. On these rivers would rise America's first and second colonial cities, New York and Philadelphia. Ironically, both of these would be on riverbanks opposite New Jersey, guaranteeing that this colony would be torn by conflicting interests and competing economies.

Nature played her hand even more strongly. In northwestern New Jersey she ranged rolling highlands and steep mountains to thwart early westward migration. To the southeast she spread a thick pine woodland over more than a million acres of soil so sandy that agricultural-minded colonists shunned it. New Jersey's long seacoast offered no inducements for settlement, for treacherous shoals and shifting currents along the offshore islands discouraged permanent residence. Behind those islands, dank sedgelands offered no inducement to stay.

Colonists thus had little choice except close to the banks of the Hudson or Delaware rivers. Later settlers followed smaller streams inland from the two main rivers. Eventually other colonists slowly filled in the twenty- to twenty-five-mile-wide strip between New York and Philadelphia, inaugurating a trend that has led to today's crowded cities and teeming highways within that corridor.

Being a peninsula unto itself did not necessarily mean that New Jersey would find a single identity (a similar peninsula just to the south is now split among Maryland, Delaware, and Virginia). Throughout much of its colonial period there was likelihood that New Jersey would be split in two, first when the Dutch and the Swedes warred over the land, and later when competing groups of Englishmen sought dominance. Its survival to statehood was difficult—and the colony did not even get its own colonial governor (as separate from rule by New York's governor) until 1738.

It was inevitable that New Jersey would become the pathway for the foot travelers, the horseback riders, and the stagecoaches moving between New York and Philadelphia and between Boston and the colonies to the south. New Jersey's taverns and inns and churches would throb with the political and religious passions that stirred an emerging nation. Here varying ideas and conflicting philosophies would meet. Since politics and religion in colonial days usually were joined, it is important to recognize that in colonial times New Jersey was home to the Dutch Reformed Church, to Presbyterians, Episcopalians, French Huguenots, Baptists, Quakers, and many other sects. Conflicting religious views clashed in this small area of limited boundaries.

New Jersey's diversification was based on wide differences in national origin. First came the Dutch and Swedes, both well settled before 1650—in different parts of New Jersey. Then the English arrived in 1664 to claim all the land. Before the Revolution, settlers arrived from Ireland, Scotland, France, Germany, and even a few from Poland and Italy. The "melting pot," so vital in all American history and in all American dreams, began in New Jersey's colonial days.

The region's temperate climate pleased varied types of settlers. Its winters were cold, but not as cold or as long as the cruel winters of New England. Its summers were warm, but not as hot or as cloying as the lazy summers of the southern colonies. Many early settlers wrote to friends in Europe of the similarity between New Jersey's seasons and the weather "back home." There could be no greater praise.

New Jersey's middle position was emphasized by nature. In the northwestern mountains, typical northern hardwood forests flourished. To the south, the pines and cedars of the so-called Pine Barrens were typical of southern woodlands. Termed "barren" by early colonists because the sandy soil would not support traditional agriculture, the Pine Barrens were far from barren. Adventurers could find plants of Canada growing side by side with plants of the Carolinas. The Pine Barrens resisted development—and still do; the pine trees and exotic plants flourish there still.

The earliest people soon found that the hoped-for silks, satins, gold, and spices of the Indies were not to be found on this peninsula. But there were other riches, especially iron in the highlands and in the pine woodlands. There was, above all, a rich soil, particularly on the riverbanks near the Delaware and Hudson rivers. This would be the basis for today's nickname: the Garden State.

New Jersey's fortunes were not to be linked solely to natural riches. They were to be tied as well to a city to the east and a city to the west. Destiny and geography linked hands across this peninsula.

J.T.C.

Wood engraving from an 1856 issue of *Ballou's Magazine* shows Henry Hudson negotiating with the Indians on the river that bears his name.

CHAPTER ONE

The Dutch and the Swedes

Although Italy played no role in New Jersey's colonial development, the first explorers to sight the peninsula were Italians—two sailing for England and the other flying a French flag. Then an Englishman's voyage in a Dutch ship gave Holland its claim to New Jersey. When Sweden entered the picture, its first ships on the Delaware River were led by the same Dutchman who had settled New Amsterdam for Holland!

It is not known whether the Italians, Giovanni (John) Caboto and his son Sebastian (called Cabot by their English employers), ever actually set foot on the land now called New Jersey. Although their second voyage for England in 1498 took them along the coast as far south as Chesapeake Bay on a commission to seek out regions "of the heathen," they left no record of going ashore. When the Cabots arrived in England, King Henry VII was so pleased with their report that he gave them a reward of ten pounds sterling "to have a good time with." Ultimately, England based its claims to all North America on the voyages of the Cabots.

The first European known to have looked carefully at New Jersey was another Italian, Giovanni da Verrazano, who sailed under the French flag in 1524. He coasted northward from Cape Fear, possibly anchoring inside both Delaware Bay and Sandy Hook Bay. He explored the lower Hudson River briefly in search of the fabled sea route to the Indies, the goal of all early explorers. France never explored this part of the New World again, preferring to penetrate North America by way of the St. Lawrence River.

Giovanni da Verrazano was the first explorer of New Jersey, according to official records. He sailed along the North American coast between North Carolina and Maine and entered New York harbor in 1524.

Hudson Explores the Coast

Henry Hudson's exploration on the Dutch ship *Half Moon* in 1609 provided the first written account of what is now New Jersey. The descriptions were recorded by Robert Juet, an English officer aboard the Dutch ship. Since much of Hudson's fame rested on Juet's journal, it is interesting to note that Juet probably kept his 1609 record as an alibi. He feared that he might be accused of being one of the mutineers who, in May of that year, near Spitsbergen, had forced Hudson to veer southwestward from the northerly course that the captain was pursuing in hopes of finding the passage to India. That 1609 sailing was Hudson's third such effort. A year later he set out on a fourth search, and in the summer of 1611 he and his son disappeared without trace when they were set adrift in Hudson Bay by a rebellious crew. Juet also was on that voyage.

The *Half Moon* followed the ocean currents in the summer of 1609 as far south as "the King's River in Virginia where our English-men are." Then Hudson turned northward to explore the coast. On August 28, 1609, he tried to pilot the *Half Moon* into "a great bay" (Delaware Bay). Despite frequent measurements of the bay's depth, "once we strooke" (went aground) before Hudson returned to the open sea and proceeded northward along the coast. The crew took frequent soundings of depths amid thunderstorms on the twenty-ninth, and Juet wrote of the Jersey shore that day and the next. He noted a stretch that seemed "to bee all Ilands to our sight" (the long string of barrier beaches now familiar to summer visitors) and the "high Hils" (today's Navesink Highlands). Juet liked what he saw: "This is a very good Land to fall with, and a pleasant Land to see."

"We saw a great fire," Juet wrote on September 2—evidence that people already lived in that dark land. Two days later, when Hudson dropped anchor inside Sandy Hook Bay, the *Half Moon*'s crew encountered some of those people. Since Hudson was seeking a passage to India, the crew optimistically believed the natives to be "Indians." The men aboard the ship were impressed by the natives, who were well-built, intelligent, and eager to please.

The Lenni-Lenape

The Indians displayed the friendliness that was a hallmark of the Lenni-Lenape Indians (meaning in their language "the Original People"). They had been on this peninsula for possibly as long as twenty thousand to thirty thousand years, after a long migration that led them from Asia to the New Jersey coast. Some modern researchers believe their wanderings may have begun in far-off Siberia. On September 4, 1609, they had their first brush with the newcomers who were to bring their downfall.

These Original People were part of the larger Algonquin nation, and English settlers often called them the Delawares rather than the Lenni-Lenape (pronounced Len-ah-pay, with slight accent on the second syllable). Within New Jersey, the Lenni-Lenape divided into three major groups: the Minsi (Men of the Stony Country) in the northern hills, the Unami (Fishermen) in the central area, and the Unilachtigo (People Living Near the Ocean) of the southern section. They had as their respective totems the wolf (Minsi), the turtle (Unami), and the wild turkey (Unilachtigo).

The Lenni-Lenape were well ordered and civilized in accordance with what they expected from life. They believed in strong family ties, with major emphasis on educating their young for the problems and challenges in the primitive environment that they must face. Boys learned to hunt and fish, to know the ways of the woodland and its wild animals; for males provided food and shelter. Female education stressed domestic chores, from gardening to the making of cornmeal, from the weaving of baskets to the making of simple garments. These Indians worshiped the sun as a giver of life and feared a god they called Manito.

The Lenni-Lenape lived chiefly in villages near the Delaware River. Their permanent homes were small, made of bark or skins stretched

A sketch belonging to the State Museum shows Indians in an everyday pursuit—hoeing corn (note baby on tree limb).

Indians hunted singly or in groups. Deer, elk, and bear were the most coveted game, and sometimes the animals were stalked for hours by hunters wearing disguises. The bow and arrow was the favorite weapon.

over bent saplings. In summer, the tribes wandered to the seacoast to gather fish or shellfish for food and seashells for wampum. That summer interlude had brought them near the Atlantic Ocean when the *Half Moon* sailed along the coast.

Peace was a passion with the Lenni-Lenape, to the extent that other Algonquin tribes sneeringly called them the Old Women. Lenni-Lenape sachems (chiefs) often brought warring tribes to the peace pipe. They offered peace to strangers—welcoming them and furnishing wayfarers with food and lodging. A perpetually boiling pot of food, to be shared with strangers, was a Lenni-Lenape custom.

Verrazano later described these Indians as "the goodliest people" that he had met on his voyage. He wrote in 1524 that they were quite tall, "the colour of brass," with quick black eyes and of "comely visage." They seemed to be "of sweet and pleasant countenance" and their women he found to be "very handsome and well favored . . . well mannered and continent as any women, and of good education."

Juet was equally impressed in 1609. He wrote on September 4:

> This day the people of the Countrey came aboord of us, seeming very glad of our comming, and brought greene Tabacco, and gave us of it for Knives and Beads. They goe in Deere skins loose, well dressed. They have yellow Copper. They desire Cloathes, and are very civill. They have great stores of Maiz or Indian Wheate, whereof they make good bread.

Two days later sailor John Colman was killed by an Indian arrow through his throat, the first recorded victim of America's Indian wars. He was buried on Sandy Hook. Natives came aboard the *Half Moon* soon after and "made a show of love" that included many gifts. Hudson and his crew felt no inclination to return the affection. The *Half Moon's* crew instead made several of the visiting Indians drunk because "they could not tell how to take it." The Indians, particularly the wives, failed to see the humor; Juet wrote with some apparent shame of one woman who "sat so modestly" in the midst of the revelry.

Hudson sailed out of Sandy Hook Bay and up the river that would bear his name, going nearly as far as present-day Albany. Late in September the *Half Moon* sailed for Holland, where Juet's journal would excite hopes of great riches. Juet wrote of "good furres," "skins of diverse sorts," and a "white greene" cliff on the west bank of the Hudson River that perhaps held either a "Copper or Silver Myne."

The Dutch Arrive

Soon, surely by 1614—and certainly long before the *Mayflower* reached Plymouth—Dutch adventurers were on Man-a-hat-ta Island ("Heavenly Land" in Indian language). At some time before 1620, some undoubtedly took a look at the western side of the Hudson, which they called the Noort (North) River, hoping to find copper or silver, for the "white greene" cliff that Juet had noted was the Palisades on the west bank. Dutch explorers combed most of the seaside of New Jersey between 1616 and 1621. They sailed up the Delaware River, calling it the

Zuydt (South) River. Captain Cornelius Jacobsz Mey explored the coast and the lower river in a series of voyages. He left at least one permanent memento; Cape May retains, in Anglicized fashion, the name that he bestowed in his own honor on New Jersey's southern cape.

The Dutch West India Company, organized in 1621, set as its two chief objectives the capture of gold-filled Spanish galleons and the establishment of a fur trade with the Indians. Since one of the company's reports recorded furs worth sixty thousand guilders and pirate plunder worth sixty million guilders, there is no question of where the early emphasis lay. Serious colonization began modestly after Captain Mey became director general of New Netherland in 1623. He dispatched a company of twenty-four men up the South (Delaware) River in 1623 to establish Fort Nassau near present-day Gloucester. Eight years later a Dutch ship followed them but found no life. The fate of the lost colonists has never been completely explained: Had they become victims

The Palisades overlooking the Hudson River still give northeastern New Jersey a formidable appearance. They look very much as they did when the first explorers saw them.

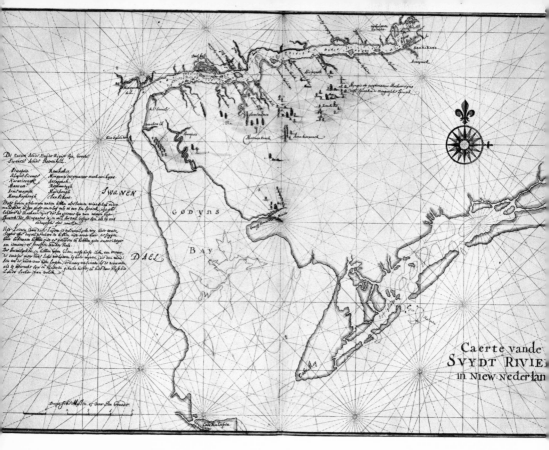

A Dutchman named J. Vingboons in 1639 drew this map of what is now southern New Jersey. It shows that the Dutch already had explored the lower Delaware River extensively. Cape May had been named.

of Indian attacks or had they wandered elsewhere? The Dutch set their sights more specifically on colonization after 1626, when Peter Minuit bought Man-a-hat-ta Island for trinkets worth twenty-four dollars (in currency of that time).

Permanent settlement was given a boost by the West India Company in 1629. Patroons who agreed to set up agricultural establishments in New Netherland were promised large tracts of land if they would place fifty immigrants "upwards of fifteen years old" on the land within four years after a holding was granted. Several patroons received land in or near what is now Jersey City, but their success was scant. There were

18

only two homes at Pavonia (named for patroon Michael Pauw) in 1633; this is part of today's Jersey City.

Pauw never settled there. He dispatched Cornelius Van Vorst with instructions to purchase the land from the Indians. Van Vorst brought with him his wife, a grown son, Jan, and several other children and grandchildren, a personal boost toward the requirement that fifty settlers occupy a patroon's land. They all settled in the salt marsh bordering the west bank of the Hudson River. Van Vorst traded so successfully with the Indians that his son Jan carried thousands of beaver skins to Holland in 1632.

Several dozen Dutch families lived on the west bank of the Hudson by 1640. One of them, Aert Teunissen Van Putten, opened one of America's first breweries in 1642. He rented his land by paying "every fourth sheaf of wheat with which God almighty shall favor the field." These Hollanders were solid families, intent on cultivating the soil and creating homes. Since their survival rested chiefly on peaceful Indians, they were dismayed in 1643 when a serious breach of faith by New Amsterdam leaders plunged the region into a disastrous war.

Midnight Massacre

William Kiefft, director general of New Netherland, ordered eighty soldiers into action on the night of February 25, 1643, to "drive away and destroy the savages" who were encamped near what is now Jersey City. Several of Kiefft's aides protested, especially Captain David DeVries, who pleaded by his own account: "Let this work alone. You will go to break the Indians, but it is our nation you are going to murder." The Dutch soldiers fell upon the sleeping Indians and murdered eighty of them before the cruel night was out. Sounds of the midnight massacre could be heard across the river, and the berserk soldiers neglected to spare even children. One account told of children slain "while fastened to their little boards."

Eleven tribes banded together to seek revenge. They struck terror into every settlement between the Raritan and Connecticut rivers. Bands of quick-moving Indians killed, burned, and looted outlying farms in a display of fury that quickly became as uncontrolled as the savage Dutch behavior that had provoked it. The Dutch sued for peace in 1645, after nearly eighteen months of Indian marauding.

Peter Stuyvesant

When Peter Stuyvesant arrived to become director general of New Netherland in May, 1647, he moved promptly to ease the tension with the Indians. He ordered Dutch conciliation toward the Indians and turned aside bursts of tribal anger with a continuing show of friendliness supported by gifts. Stuyvesant pleaded that "Christians carefully abstain from betraying any desire of revenge."

Peter Stuyvesant was the son of a minister. University trained, he had joined the Dutch West India Company in 1632. He was assigned to Curaçao in the Netherlands Antilles, where he rose to governor and in 1643 lost his right leg in an island battle. The next year he returned to Holland to be fitted for the well-known wooden leg, which he wore for the rest of his life. He was thirty-seven years old when he was named director general of New Netherland. As he stomped down the gangplank to take control, he pledged that he would be "as a father over his children."

Stuyvesant's strict, autocratic rule was what he deemed necessary to cope with harsh frontier existence. He forced his villagers to bare their heads when they stood before him. When his councilors opposed his bullying, Stuyvesant told them: "We derive our authority from God and the Company, not from a few ignorant subjects." Settlers called him "Old Peg Leg" behind his back, but they came at least to respect his relentless will to strengthen Dutch colonization. There is nothing to indicate they ever loved him as a father.

Stuyvesant recognized a danger greater than Indian warfare. Other nations were making overtures along the South River. Proof of long-standing dispute over the river was evident in the fact that the stream was also commonly known as the Delaware River. It was so named in 1610 by Captain Samuel Argall of England, who sailed up the river and

Peter Stuyvesant, the strong-minded governor of New Netherland, which included modern New Jersey.

claimed it for the British. He named it for Lord De La Warre, Governor of Virginia. Four years later Argall anchored off Man-a-hat-ta Island to demand that the three or four Dutch settlers swear loyalty to England. They agreed and promised to pay tribute. The promise was forgotten as soon as Argall's sails disappeared over the horizon.

But by Stuyvesant's time the Dutch had genuine reason for concern. For one thing, in the 1630's settlers from New England had established a small colony along the river at Varkens Kill, not far from today's town of Salem. More important, Sweden had chosen the Delaware River for its only American colonizing attempt. By 1647 the Swedes were a persistent, if ill-equipped, threat. Stuyvesant recognized that there was no room for coexistence on the river. He decided that the Swedes must be pushed aside.

New Sweden

New Sweden had begun officially in mid-March, 1638, when two ships, the *Kalmar Nyckel* and the *Vogel Grip*, limped into Delaware Bay after a fierce Atlantic crossing that had taken more than ten weeks.

HILLSBOROUGH TWP. PUBLIC LIBRARY ASSOCIATION

Commanding the expedition was an unlikely Swedish colonizer: Peter Minuit—who in 1626 had bought Man-a-hat-ta Island from the Indians for the Dutch! Minuit had high hopes for New Sweden, although his twenty-five original colonists were soldiers, not likely candidates to settle down to domesticity in a new country.

Minuit apparently slipped into Delaware Bay by subterfuge. He stopped at Fort Nassau to tell the Dutch he was headed for the West Indies but needed to replenish his wood and water supplies. "Some time afterwards," according to the Dutch account, "some of our people going again found the Swedes still there, but then they had already made a small garden for raising salads, pot herbs and the like. They wondered at this and inquired of the Swedes what it meant and whether they intended to stay here." The Swedes calmly built Fort Christina at what is now Wilmington, Delaware. The Dutch issued protests, "but they have as much effect as the flying of a crow overhead."

That sort of paper warfare characterized a long, strange struggle be-

Johan Printz, governor of New Sweden. A giant of a man, he was both respected and hated by his colonists. He built Fort Elfsborg in what is now New Jersey's Salem County. For several years the Swedish fort controlled the lower Delaware River.

tween the Dutch and the Swedes. Neither really knew what to do about the other, and neither had the power to do anything. New Sweden suffered from lack of homeland support, unquestionably because of the early loss of Peter Minuit, the very heart and soul of New Sweden. Minuit boarded the *Kalmar Nyckel* in the fall of 1638 and sailed for the West Indies. While he was in port there, a hurricane struck, and Minuit perished when his ship went down in the gale winds. New Sweden's chief source of strength was gone.

Minuit's successor was Peter Hollander Ridder, another Dutchman in Swedish service. Ridder hoped to find Swedish people eager to sail for a new life in America, but he found no such enthusiasm. Instead, he brought with him people forced to leave Sweden, including army deserters and several prisoners. Another shipload of colonists in 1641 included a few Finns as well as Swedes whose financial or ethical difficulties had forced them to leave home. Ridder complained that it "would be impossible to find more stupid people in all Sweden." Not one of them could build "a common peasant's house," he said. Ridder was recalled early in 1643.

Johan Printz

New Sweden achieved its only stature when one of colonial America's most flamboyant and controversial characters arrived in 1643 as Ridder's replacement. He was Johan Printz, who, with a background similar in many ways to that of Peter Stuyvesant, was destined to become "Old Peg Leg's" chief adversary. The son of a Swedish clergyman, Printz had been educated for a professional life. Instead, he entered military service, where he won considerable distinction in the West Gotha Cavalry Regiment. He had become a lieutenant colonel and had been knighted just before his appointment as governor of New Sweden. The fifty-one-year-old governor brought with him his wife and five daughters as proof of his determination to make his home in New Sweden.

Printz was a man to be reckoned with. Contemporary accounts said that he weighed four hundred pounds and stood nearly seven feet tall.

His friends acknowledged that he was severe and strict but a zealous defender of Sweden's interests. His enemies called him cruel, arbitrary, dictatorial, choleric, extravagant, and unpleasant. Printz combined all these traits, all necessary if New Sweden was to survive in the midst of unceasing pressures from the Dutch. He set about to salvage what he could from the feeble colonizing efforts of his predecessors.

New Sweden was centered near present-day Wilmington when Printz arrived. Only a few settlers had ventured across to the New Jersey side of the Delaware River. A count in 1644 showed only 121 people scattered through all of New Sweden, vaguely encompassing parts of modern Pennsylvania and Delaware as well as southwestern New Jersey. Only seventeen were on the east bank of the river, most of them at Fort Elfsborg.

Fort Elfsborg deserves at least a footnote in history. Printz began building it immediately after his arrival. He chose a high promontory several miles below the Varkens Kill (now the Salem River), commanding a view of the river for several miles in both directions. Its guns were high enough to make Dutch commanders wary, and threatening enough to force the English settlers at Varkens Kill to swear allegiance to New Sweden. Printz thus added about one hundred subjects to his little empire, even if their loyalty was open to question. Soldiers at the fort lived in daily boredom, since few Dutch ships ever passed by. Worse, the persistent Delaware Bay mosquitoes attacked day and night. Infuriated by this implacable foe, Swedish soldiers dubbed the fort *Myggenborg* or "Mosquito Castle."

The Swedes and the Dutch settled down to a wary struggle noteworthy for its lack of action. Printz scrupulously maintained peace with the soldiers at Fort Nassau by switching to cajolery when his subtle insults irked the Dutch. He kept them off balance by insisting that the English colonists at Varkens Kill and the Indians were potentially more threatening than New Sweden's guns.

Printz despised the Indians, writing at one time that if he had more soldiers, "with the help of God not a single savage would be allowed to live on this river." For their part, the Indians among themselves mockingly referred to Printz as "Big Tub" or "Big Belly." But despite their understandable dislike of the governor and his coolness toward them, the Indians sold Printz enough grain to see his beleaguered colonists through several severe winters.

Printz needed all his wits to cope with his foes. Sweden sent little help. Once a stretch of five years went by without a single ship from home. On the rare occasion that a ship did come, chances were it brought such frivolities as brandy and fishhooks, and—in one case—gilded flagpole knobs. Printz's troubles mounted after 1651, when Governor Stuyvesant decided that the time had come to put an end to Swedish pretensions. He personally led 120 men overland to strengthen Fort Nassau in 1651 and simultaneously sent eleven ships around the cape in a show of naval power. Later that year Stuyvesant built Fort Casimir on the west bank of the Delaware at a place called Santhoeck, downstream from Fort Christina. Outflanked, Printz withdrew his troops from Fort Elfsborg, leaving it to the mosquitoes and the lashing tides.

Time had run out for Printz by the spring of 1653. He had not seen a Swedish ship since 1648, a too-poignant reminder of his diminished status at home. He decided to leave, and so limited was available shipping that he had to walk across the peninsula to New Amsterdam, leading his wife and four of his daughters (one daughter remained in New Sweden, married to a settler). Twenty other disaffected colonists joined the Printzes. At New Amsterdam, the Swedes sailed for home aboard a Dutch vessel, a sad punctuation to what had been a Swedish dream. New Sweden's collapse was just a matter of time.

Farewell to New Sweden

Ironically, New Sweden received its only determined burst of colonizing activity just after Printz's departure. The New Sweden Company finally sent out 260 colonists in 1654—nearly four times the number in America after sixteen years of previous colonial effort! A year later the ship *Mercurius* sailed from Sweden, packed with settlers and leaving behind on the docks another hundred people who vowed they would sail on the next ship. New Sweden came alive just as it died.

When the *Mercurius* arrived in Delaware Bay, there no longer was a New Sweden. The sequence of events that led to complete Dutch take-over was precipitated chiefly because Printz's successor, Governor Johan Rising, unwittingly broke the unwritten rule between the Dutch and the Swedes that neither would genuinely press hostilities on the Delaware. Printz's blustering had been accepted as such by the Dutch. Stuyvesant's outflanking of Fort Christina by the building of Fort Casimir posed no aggressive threat. As long as neither side upset the delicate balance of the gentlemen's agreement, there would be no violence. The new governor violated the agreement by doing exactly what seemed logical.

On the way up the river on May 21, 1654, inbound from Sweden, Rising dropped anchor before the guns of Fort Casimir and fired his ship's cannon in salute. Then, according to one of his officers, he sent "four files of musketeers to the Holland command . . . to demand delivery of the said fort." The Dutch haggled despite "a couple of shots from our heaviest guns," then capitulated. The Swedes "took possession of their guns and cannon," and raised the Swedish banner over the fort. They re-named it Fort Trinity, "because it was captured on Trinity Sunday."

Stuyvesant could not tolerate such effrontery. He put 317 soldiers aboard several ships and sailed from New Amsterdam to Fort Casimir in September, 1655. The Swedes forgot their valor of Trinity Sunday and surrendered without wasting any gunpowder. Stuyvesant proceeded up-river and after a few days of desultory siege forced Fort Christina's surrender. New Sweden had passed forever into history. Most of its settlers chose to stay. Since they had a lower-class status in Sweden or Finland, they were better off in America, no matter who ruled.

The influence of the Swedes on the lower Delaware continued. For at least another century, Swedish names and Swedish customs dominated major portions of Gloucester County. The town of Raccoon (now Swedesboro) became a major center of Swedish thought, centered on a Swedish church where all records were kept in Swedish for decades and

A portion of this home in the Pine Barrens of southern New Jersey is said to date back more than three hundred years to the days of New Sweden. An important Swedish contribution to colonial America was the log cabin. This is an etching by Earl Horter in the State Library.

where gravestones told of large Swedish families. The loyalty of these Scandinavians was to the land rather than to specific flags.

Perhaps the most unusual Swedish contribution to American life was the log cabin, generally associated with later pioneer settlements in the forests beyond the Allegheny Mountains. The colonial Swedes built houses of cedar logs, notching the ends for tight fit and filling the chinks with locally made mortar. Many such houses are known to have formerly existed in New Jersey, Pennsylvania, and Delaware. One still stands behind the brick Hancock House at Hancock's Bridge in Salem County, moved there from its previous location.

But the relics of New Sweden, which was about to know yet another conqueror, are very few indeed. We can still find Swedish names on headstones in graveyards at Swedesboro, Churchtown, and Friesburg. Repaupo boasts the tradition of being "the most Swedish" of all New Jersey towns. Beautiful old Swede's Church is a landmark in Swedesboro—although it was built after the Revolution, by which time the

27

original Swedish name of Raccoon had been changed to Swedesboro. The Maurice and Mullica rivers perpetuate the names of early Scandinavian settlers. The contribution of the Swedes has been best memorialized by historian Adrian C. Leiby, who wrote in 1964:

> Overwhelmed by numbers of English, German and Scotch Irish neighbors, it would be hard to trace to the Swedes of New Jersey any distinct contributions to the ways of America. It would be hard too, to find a trace of any branch of the Delaware in the main stream, yet no thoughtful person will doubt that it is there.

Indian Raid

Stuyvesant could not have changed the customs and habits of Swedish settlers, nor is it likely that he wished to do so. The most precious commodity in that frontier land was people, regardless of nationality or customs, to man the outposts and battle the forests. Stuyvesant had to forget the Swedes under any circumstances. He had trouble enough in New Amsterdam in the fall of 1655, for while he was subduing the Swedes, the Indians had started to war again.

Manhattan Islanders faced a tense situation on September 15, 1655, when about five hundred heavily armed Indians tied up their canoes on the banks. The visitors walked threateningly through the town streets and even strode boldly into homes. They withdrew at the end of the day, leaving New Amsterdam people to face an uneasy night. Shortly after 9 P.M., Schout (sheriff) Hendrick Van Dyke shot and killed a young Indian girl who allegedly had been raiding his peach orchard. The next day Dutch soldiers attacked the Indians, killing three of them and driving the rest into their canoes and across the Hudson River to the New Jersey side.

The Indians put the torch to the land. That evening flames pierced the darkness across the river, beginning at Maryn Adriansen's house in Hoboken, then engulfing other nearby Dutch farmhouses. Every building in Hoboken, Pavonia, and Communipaw (two parts of modern Jersey City) was destroyed before morning, and everybody that lived there had been either killed or captured. A thousand more warriors joined the rampage. Within three days the Indians burned out everything on the west bank of the Hudson and in much of Staten Island. About 100 settlers were killed and more than 150 persons, mostly women and children, were captured. Five to six hundred head of cattle were either killed or captured.

Stuyvesant reached Manhattan after the flames had died and the killings had ceased. He spurned all suggestions of counterattack and secured a quick truce that ensured the safe return of the prisoners. He instituted stringent regulations for those who would settle beyond the guns of Fort Amsterdam. All inhabitants along the west side of the river were ordered to "settle themselves together in the form of towns, villages, or hamlets like our neighbors of New England." Failure to comply would bring an immediate fine of twenty-five guilders a year. The governor also banned straw roofs and wooden chimneys as a precaution against Indian fire raids.

Settlers went back across the river and resumed their old ways in defiance of both Indian dangers and Stuyvesant's wrath. The governor sent out soldiers in February, 1660, to spread a warning that anyone who had not removed "houses, goods, and cattle" to the "village or settlement nearest or most convenient by the end of March or at the latest, the middle of April," would suffer "the pain of confistication." That was a doubly harsh expectation, for the time to comply was short—and there were no villages at all on the west bank, convenient or otherwise.

New Jersey's First Town

Threats of "confistication" partially succeeded. New Jersey's first official town was established in August, 1660, as the result of Stuyvesant's order. A village called Bergen was laid out around a square that was 800 feet on each side. Two streets crossing in the middle divided the square

A sketch made for the tercentenary celebration of New Jersey's birthday in 1664 shows the village of Bergen as it looked when the English took over.

into quarters. An area 165 feet by 225 feet in the center was dedicated to community use, and the entire village was surrounded by tall wooden barricades. Outside lay the *buynten tuyn* or "outside gardens," where villagers raised their vegetables or herded their cows by day. All cattle were driven back to the town square at nightfall and the gates were closed. Old Bergen has been swallowed up in modern Jersey City, but its original outlines are preserved in the border streets of today's Bergen Square.

Most Dutchmen took Stuyvesant's directive lightly, believing that in a wilderness country, distance protected them from fines or confiscation of property. They established a series of outposts along the Hackensack River that later became towns, including the town of Hackensack. Others ventured far up the Raritan River, founding such towns as New Brunswick, Millstone, and Somerville.

Copper from the Wilderness

The most adventurous Dutchmen of all went astoundingly far away. They sailed up the Hudson River about 1640 to Esopus (now Kingston, New York), and then proceeded southwestward on foot through what was described as "a howling wilderness." They found a thick lode of copper in the Kittatinny Mountains near the Delaware Water Gap, sank shafts to dig it, and then built a 104-mile-long roadway from the mine to Esopus. By the middle 1650's the Dutch were carrying enough copper ore along this Old Mine Road to sustain their interest for many years.

The copper ore was placed on ships at Esopus and taken to New Amsterdam and then to Holland for refining. This was a most astounding venture, particularly when one views the area today, more than three centuries after the Dutch found and successfully mined the copper. The entrance to the old mine can still be seen on land owned by a Boy Scout camp in the least settled part of New Jersey. The old road, only moderately improved, still exists as a two-car macadam route through some of the most rugged areas of New Jersey and New York.

The Old Octagonal Church that stood in the old Dutch town of Bergen in present-day Jersey City. It was the first church built in New Jersey.

Those copper-digging Dutchmen lived and worked in the heart of an area inhabited by the Minsi tribe, supposedly the most aggressive of the Lenni-Lenape Indians. But there is no record of Indian trouble. The copper workers ignored Stuyvesant more and more. Old documents show that in 1659 they took their ore directly to Holland without even informing the governor, much less asking his permission. As for the rest of the world, they just let it go by. It would be a full century before other settlers would push westward over the forbidding mountain barriers between the Pahaquarry mine and New Amsterdam sixty miles to the east. New Amsterdam was almost a forgotten name by the time others came to dwell in the valley of the copper mines.

By the time of the American Revolution, the long road to Esopus, rather than the copper, had become important. Troops moving through western New Jersey traversed it, and President John Adams often used the road as a handy shortcut between Philadelphia and his home in Massachusetts. The road is destined soon to disappear beneath the waters of the proposed Tocks Island Reservoir.

A Prosperous Colony

New Netherland was growing and prosperous along both the Hudson and Delaware rivers as the 1660's went by. Holland sent out hundreds of settlers each year. Some of those sent to the Delaware settlements were children of the Amsterdam almshouse, prompting Stuyvesant to write home that "none ought to come if less than fifteen years of age and somewhat strong." The governor was irked by the laziness of some of New Amsterdam's newcomers. Stuyvesant complained that they refused to do any work during the "blessed year," a time of grace that they claimed was due them under the terms of their emigration agreements.

New Amsterdam's fine harbor already was winning the shipping importance that later would carry New York to international prominence. Vessels came and went with some frequency, with an occasional booty-laden privateer ship mixed among the regular merchant vessels. The

The Dutch gave to northeastern New Jersey the characteristic "Dutch" look. The shape of the houses is really Flemish, but the gambrel roof is typical of many homes found in northeastern New Jersey, where the Dutch settled. The houses are usually of stone.

privateers usually anchored on the New Jersey side of the river, where there was less fussiness about the cargoes and the crews.

By 1660 the Dutch settlements also included many types of people other than Protestant Dutchmen, including French Huguenots, Germans, a few Jews, and a number of Negroes. The latter were in town as early as 1629, when a gang of them were imported to build Fort Amsterdam. One Negro, who might have been the first black in New Jersey, was a gift to Jacob Stoffelson of Ahimus (Jersey City) from Captain Geurt Tyson, a noted privateer, who dropped anchor by Stoffelson's plantation. Dutchmen along the Delaware also had many Negro slaves, perhaps more than their relatives on the banks of the Hudson.

Holland's greatest contribution was the sturdy colonists who so loved the land that they were willing to spend long years clearing the forests and tilling the soil. America was their new homeland, although they remained Dutch and continued to speak Old World Dutch even after conquest. (Several communities in Bergen County kept official town records in Dutch until the middle of the nineteenth century.) In time they built the big stone "Dutch" houses that are scattered throughout Bergen County and in parts of Morris and Somerset. In time, too, they built the sturdy stone churches, such as the one on the Hackensack Green. The chief Dutch contribution to the history and culture of New Jersey was the establishment of Queen's College in New Brunswick in 1766—102 years after England claimed all of New Jersey. Queen's changed its name to Rutgers College early in the nineteenth century and now has become Rutgers, the State University, with more than thirty thousand students.

Since they had large families, Dutch names still abound in the northeastern part of the state. Here are many members of the distinguished Frelinghuysen family, noted for its civic and political leaders through more than two centuries. Here are the Van Dorens, Van Duynes, and Cowenhovens (or Conovers). Here are the Westervelts and Bogerts and Van Houtens and Blauvelts. There is no question that the Dutch were here, and that they were blessed with many sons.

Stuyvesant should have had time to savor the pleasures of this most prosperous center in the New World. But circumstances were moving to number his days as governor of New Netherland. By spring of 1664, an English fleet was on the high seas, bound for the New World. Stuyvesant may have heard that it had embarked, but Holland's leaders were sure it was headed for New England. They could not possibly have conceived that its destination was New Amsterdam. Stuyvesant's shock in August, when alien ships anchored in the harbor, must have been nearly as great as that of the Indians who saw the Dutch *Half Moon* off the New Jersey shore fifty-five years before. The Dutch ruler was a wise man; he knew that his power in the New World would now be measured in hours, not years.

CHAPTER TWO

The East of New Jersey

Gazing glumly outward at the four British ships anchored in the Hudson River in mid-August, 1664, Peter Stuyvesant was as astonished as he was appalled. Stuyvesant naturally had accepted the word of homeland military experts that the fleet had been bound only for New England. Yet out there on the Hudson lay the four ships, British flags unfurled on the masts and cannons at battle-ready on the decks.

In that era of slow sea-borne communications, Stuyvesant of course did not know of England's closely kept decision that it would no longer tolerate a Dutch colony flourishing midway between the English settlements in New England and Virginia. The return of King Charles II to the British throne had restored England's colonial ambitions. England could turn its attention to the colonization of America—peacefully, if possible; at the end of a sword, if need be. There were strong feelings of rivalry between the English and the Dutch at the time, and both nations had long struggled for dominance in world trade and colonial expansion.

King Charles completely ignored Dutch claims to New Netherland when he summoned his "Dearest Brother" James, the Duke of York, on March 12, 1664, and granted him all the land between the Connecticut and Delaware rivers. "Dearest Brother" was granted the right to wrest whatever fortune he could from the land, as well as the power to govern as "he shall thinke to be fittest for the good of the Adventurers & Inhabitants there." That included everyone—Dutch, Swedes, Indians, and anyone else who might be in the area.

James, Duke of York. In March of 1664 he was given the area now including New Jersey by his brother, King Charles II.

The Duke of York, in turn, promptly chose Colonel Robert Nicolls to subdue the territory in the name of England and the Duke. Nicolls sailed secretly in May with 450 men aboard his four vessels, instructed to stop first in New England. There he could supplement his forces with volunteers, if he needed them, to attack New Amsterdam. The Duke commissioned Nicolls as his deputy governor, with full power to act. That commission, combined with another seemingly offhanded action by the Duke, would woefully tangle the affairs of a New Jersey just about to be created.

The Transfer of New Jersey

Nicolls was far out on the Atlantic on June 23, 1664, when the Duke of York generously—and carelessly—split his holdings. He gave two court favorites, Sir George Carteret and John, Lord Berkeley, all the peninsula that lay between the Hudson and Delaware rivers. James asked little in return. He would get only ten shillings "in hand payd" and "Twentie Nobles of Lawfull money" per year. In addition, Berkeley and Carteret were liable for "the rent of a pepper corne upon the Feast of the Nativity of St. John Baptist next ensueing if the same shall be lawfully demanded." New Jersey officially began its existence that June day, both geographically and politically, for the Duke of York decreed in his grant that the "said Tract of land hereafter is to be called by the name or names of New Cesarea or New Jersey."

The name New Jersey was a matter of deeply felt sentiment. The Duke chose it to express his gratitude to Sir George Carteret, who had been born on the Isle of Jersey off the coast of England. Carteret had stoutly defended this British outpost against Cromwell forces in the English Civil War that had temporarily unseated the ruling Stuart family in the 1640's and resulted in the execution of King Charles I.

Robert Nicolls Takes Over

Nicolls knew nothing of that sentimental court maneuvering when he dropped anchor at New Amsterdam in August and ordered Stuyvesant to surrender or fight. The aging Dutch governor at first wanted to defend his colony, but he heeded the pleas of ninety-three of the settlement's leading citizens that New Amsterdam would be ruined by a long siege. When they urged surrender, Stuyvesant said, "Let it be so." He stalled for more than a week to gain the best possible terms, then ordered the white flag of surrender raised on August 27. Stuyvesant was reported to have said sadly, "I had rather be carried to my grave." Then he left the fort, with Dutch banners flying over the troops that followed him out.

Nicolls renamed the town New York in honor of the Duke. He dispatched his military aide, Sir Robert Carr, to subdue the Dutch and Swedish settlements on the Delaware River. Carr met no opposition, but with an unnecessary show of strength he turned his soldiers loose on Fort Amstel (at what is now New Castle, Delaware), killing several settlers. In Carr's own words, "the soldiers never stopping until they stormed ye fort, and soe consequently to plundering: the seamen, noe less given to that sporte, were quickly within, & have gotten a good store of booty." Carr divided the remaining spoils with officers of his staff, giving them houses, land, Negro slaves, and other possessions taken from the Dutch. He reserved for himself a large Dutch estate on Burlington Island and lived there for more than a year.

Carr's plundering disturbed Nicolls, who has been described by historian John Fiske as "one of the most genial and attractive figures in early American history." Nicolls took very seriously his appointment as the Duke of York's governor and saw himself as a peaceful colonizer, not a conqueror. He offered such amnesty to the Dutch settlers that they felt that their personal rights were better protected than ever before. Even Peter Stuyvesant chose to live out his years on Manhattan Island. He made a brief visit to Holland to clear his record on the defense of New Amsterdam, then returned "home" to America.

Nicolls recognized that this great open land would be of little consequence unless new settlers could be attracted. He decided to seek people from New England, correctly guessing that many restless families there might be seeking to move on after a generation or two of life in Massachusetts, Connecticut, or elsewhere (and in fact many New Englanders already had relocated in Long Island). Governor Nicolls issued a broadside inviting Englishmen in other parts of America "to set out a town and inhabit together in Albania," as he called New Jersey. Within two years six such towns were established by families relocated from New England or Long Island—Elizabethtown, Middletown, Shrewsbury, Newark, Woodbridge, and Piscataway.

Prospective settlers were granted a somewhat limited freedom of worship by Nicolls, "provided such liberty is not carried to licentiousness or the disturbance of others in the exercise of the Protestant religion." Nicolls guaranteed inhabitants the right to tax themselves and declared that settlers could get land simply by applying to him for permission to purchase "from Indians of the projected location." Nicolls'

Good Order Established

IN

Pennsilvania & New-Jersey

IN

AMERICA,

Being a true Account of the Country;
With its Produce and Commodities there made.

And the great Improvements that may be made by
means of **Publick Store-houses** for **Hemp,**
Flax and **Linnen-Cloth**; also, the Advantages
of a **Publick-School**, the Profits of a **Publick-**
Bank, and the Probability of its arising, if those
directions here laid down are followed. With
the advantages of publick **Granaries.**

Likewise, several other things needful to be understood by those that are or do intend to be concerned in planting in the said Countries.

All which is laid down very plain, in this small
Treatise; it being easie to be understood by any
ordinary Capacity. To which the *Reader* is
referred for his further satisfaction.

By Thomas Budd.

Printed in the Year 1685.

A

FURTHER ACCOUNT

OF

New JERSEY,

In an Abstract of

LETTERS

Lately Writ from thence,

By several Inhabitants there Resident.

Printed in the Year 1676.

New Jersey's attractions for settlers became the subject of several brochures printed in England to encourage residents to settle there. Two of them are this "Further Account of New Jersey," published in 1676, and the glowing account that Thomas Budd wrote in 1685 on "Good Order Established in Pennsylvania & New Jersey." The Budd book was printed in Philadelphia, but its primary purpose was to attract emigrants from England.

stipulations regarding taxes and easy land purchases would cause bitterness and bloodshed for nearly a full century to come.

The Founding of Elizabeth and Monmouth

Two groups of Long Islanders, both transplants from New England, quickly accepted Nicolls' terms. Four "Associates" from Jamaica, Long Island, asked the governor on September 25, 1664, for permission to settle west of the Achter Kol (a Dutch name meaning the "after kill" or "back stream"), the waterway that divided Staten Island from New Jersey (the Arthur Kill). A month later, Luke Watson, John Ogden, John Bailey, and John Baker purchased from the Indians a huge section

39

between the Raritan and Passaic rivers and extending some thirty miles inland. Today this is New Jersey's most settled region; in 1664 it was a thickly forested wilderness. The Associates paid the Indians "twenty fathoms of trading cloth, two made coats, two guns, two kettles, ten bars of lead and twenty handfuls of powder" for their land.

Nicolls gave another Long Island group permission in the spring of 1665 to negotiate with the Indians for most of modern Monmouth County. They purchased a tract about twelve miles wide, vaguely described as running from Sandy Hook westward to the south side of Raritan Bay. The payment included a peculiar provision that the Indians could continue to harvest beach plums on Sandy Hook. Nicolls guaranteed Monmouth settlers full religious freedom and the right to hold a representative assembly. The religious freedom was not taken as empty gesture. Baptists from Rhode Island founded Middletown and Quakers from Gravesend, Long Island, settled Shrewsbury.

Mischief again was on the high seas in that spring of 1665. Berkeley and Carteret decided to capitalize on their holdings in New Jersey, knowing nothing of Nicolls' land grants or his liberal terms to settlers. They named Philip Carteret, a distant cousin of Sir George, governor of New Jersey on February 10, 1665, and dispatched him to rule their holdings. They also ordered him to collect an annual rent of a halfpenny an acre—although the rents would not be due before 1670, in what Berkeley and Carteret undoubtedly felt would be regarded by colonists as a warm gesture of friendship. Governor Carteret, twenty-six years old and scarcely wise in the ways of politics or real estate, reached New York in July, 1665, aboard the ship *Philip*.

Philip Carteret

Happy with his own type of colonizing, Nicolls was dazed by Philip Carteret's arrival. Till this point he knew nothing of the curious land deal of June, 1664. Nicolls dispatched a furious letter to the Duke of York, sharply scolding him for parting with Albania, as he continued to call New Jersey. That land west of the Hudson River contained all the "most improveablest part" of the Duke's holdings, Nicolls wrote. It "could receive twenty times more people than Long Island" and had "the fair hope of Rich mines."

Carteret did not tarry long in the company of the furious governor of New York. He reboarded the *Philip*, sailed it westward beyond Staten Island, and late in July anchored offshore at Achter Kol, as the emerging riverbank village apparently was known. Tradition says that there were only four families on hand; modern historians believe that more settlers probably had joined the families of the original four Associates by July, 1665. But even if there had been only the original Associate families, the population total would have been quite respectable because of John Ogden. He had brought with him to Achter Kol his wife and five sons, ranging in age from twelve to twenty-six. Sturdy sons, in colonial times, constituted wealth of the highest magnitude.

Carteret had come to stay. With him aboard the *Philip* were about thirty men and women from the Isle of Jersey. Eighteen were servants, whose presence indicated that Carteret anticipated a luxurious life in New Jersey. Carteret's followers were either Roman Catholics or members of the Church of England. Such religious leanings could not endear them to the relocated New England Puritans. For their part, the newcomers, presumably all loyal to the royal family, must have realized that these Puritans had been pleased when Cromwell had temporarily unseated the Stuarts.

So they faced one another on the shore: newcomers who perhaps hoped for something akin to ease, and the rugged transplants who hoped to found still another Puritan stronghold. Carteret came ashore to manifest his right to rule and he must have displayed good manners as well as a conciliatory attitude.

Tradition says that Philip Carteret explained the transfer of New Jersey to Lord Berkeley and Sir George Carteret and read the commission naming him governor of the province. He then outlined a liberal charter called *The Concessions and Agreements*, wherein rights customarily belonging to free Englishmen at home were bestowed on all those settling within New Jersey. The Associates countered by describing their property rights under Governor Nicolls' terms and showed their land deed signed by Indian sachems. Carteret surely pointed out that the rights of the proprietors, under the grant from the Duke, preceded the Indian deed by five months.

The meeting must have been amicable enough. To dramatize his dual role as a new settler and the governor, Carteret is said to have shouldered a hoe and marched up to the village. Behind him trooped the settlers, old and new; some dressed in frontier homespun and others in the garb of the Isle of Jersey. Achter Kol was renamed Elizabethtown in honor of Sir George Carteret's wife. About a month after his arrival, Philip Carteret became one of the Elizabethtown Associates by buying the rights of John Bailey, who had decided not to settle beside the Achtor Kol. By deed, at least, he recognized the Nicolls' grant.

Carteret knew that Nicolls was no friend. He was also worried that Indians might attack the ill-defended community. On August 2, 1666, Carteret wrote to the proprietors in England that New York interests desired to see Elizabethtown fail, to the extent that "one of their greatest hopes [is] that the Indians would not suffer us to inhabit here." Envious New Yorkers, he complained, had told him that they would not sell him ammunition or even send help in case of Indian attack.

Connecticut Puritans Come to New Jersey

Other New Englanders set their sights on New Jersey, since Nicolls' earlier invitation had been reinforced by a later broadside that Carteret's men distributed throughout New England. Puritans in the Connecticut coastal towns of Branford and Milford sent Captain Robert Treat of Milford, then forty-one years old and a veteran of New England's Indian wars, to Elizabethtown in the fall of 1665 to confer with the new governor of New Jersey. Carteret cordially urged Treat to look over the province. The Milford captain first explored along the Delaware River, then part of Carteret's domain, before deciding that a site closer to Connecticut would be more pleasant.

Treat represented a band of Puritans who had been continually disenchanted wherever they went. They had most recently been disturbed by the uniting of the Connecticut and New Haven colonies, feeling that the union threatened their theological liberties. Religious freedom to the Milford and Branford Puritans did not mean respect for differing theologies. Rather it meant the right to practice *their* religion, without any interference from those they considered less devout than they were. Whenever they had suspected pressures from others, they had moved on. Most of those in the two Connecticut shore towns had been moving about for years, even decades, in search of a perfect place where they might be beyond the corruption of conflicting opinions.

A typical example of these Puritans was the Reverend Abraham Pierson, the religious leader of Branford. A graduate of England's Cambridge University, he had emigrated to Boston in 1639. Within a year he moved on to Lynn, Massachusetts, then took a small group of people to Southold, Long Island, and eventually on to Southampton, Long Island. Everywhere they went he and his followers sought a Puritan utopia; always they were disappointed. Pierson and his flock had left

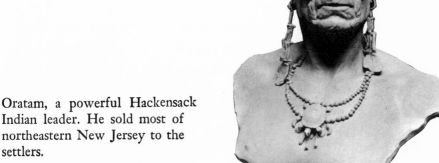

Oratam, a powerful Hackensack Indian leader. He sold most of northeastern New Jersey to the settlers.

43

Mural in the Robert Treat Hotel shows Robert Treat dickering with the Indians in 1667 about the purchase of the present site of the city of Newark.

Long Island for Branford, and by 1665 that had become less than ideal to their way of thinking. The migratory life of Mr. Pierson and his wife was evident in the birthplaces of their eight children: one born in Lynn, three on Long Island, and four in Branford.

Robert Treat finally chose a New Jersey location on the Passaic River where it met a broad bay just to the north of Elizabethtown. Sweet green marsh grasses grew on the banks of the deep stream, which led inland to perfect seclusion. Treat agreed to bring his followers there the next spring if Carteret cleared land titles. The next May, Treat led thirty Milford families down Long Island Sound to New Jersey and four miles inland on the Passaic River. A band of Indians awaited them, but not as a welcoming party. They refused to let the colonists land until they had paid for their land.

Treat reacted angrily. His first impulse was to return to Connecticut, but the boats drifted downwind to Elizabethtown, where Carteret hastily supplied an interpreter and a guide to lead Treat to Indian headquarters. Terms were arranged for the land, and the Puritans later paid the Indians "fifty double hands of powder, one hundred barrs of lead, twenty Axes,

44

twenty coates, ten Guns, twenty pistolls, ten kettles, ten Swords, four blankets, four barrells of beere, ten pair of breeches, fifty knives, twenty howes, eight hundred and fifty fathom of wampum, two Ankors of Licquers or something Equivolent and three troopers Coates."

That miscellany bought the Puritans nearly all of modern Essex County. It scarcely represented true value, but the Indians apparently did not know they were selling the land itself. To them the woods and fields were free and open, theirs neither to own nor to sell. Perhaps they believed they were selling only hunting and fishing territories. For legal-minded Englishmen, however, property and signed deeds were synonymous.

Newark Is Founded

The settlers first named their new town Milford, then Newark in honor of Newark-on-Trent, the English birthplace of Mr. Pierson, the town's spiritual guide. Newark's civil leader was Treat, who contributed not only his military experience and solid colonizing wisdom but also brought to Newark his eight children, ranging in age from three to fifteen. By June 27, 1667, when family heads from Milford and Branford signed a compact that affirmed the power of the church in all civic as well as religious matters, there were about 350 people in Newark. Few American towns had such a quick initial settlement.

Two other towns were begun in 1666 by relocated New Englanders. Governor Carteret signed an agreement on May 21 to establish Woodbridge and Piscataway, each about eight miles square. Woodbridge settlers came from the vicinity of Newbury, Massachusetts; they took their town name from the Reverend John Woodbridge, who was both the minister and the judge in the town named in his honor. Piscataway's founders from near the Piscataqua River in Maine transferred the river name to their town in New Jersey. As time went by, it became Piscataway.

All six new towns founded under Nicolls or Carteret adhered to New

England patterns, which meant it was assumed that each town had the privilege and the duty of supplying all its citizens' needs. The closely knit towns centered on a meetinghouse that served in many ways: as a center of worship, a place for town meetings, a school, and, in case of emergency, as a fort. Land was divided by lottery, except in a few cases where large plots were reserved for leaders, who were not required to participate in the drawings. (Robert Treat, for example, was given outright a choice six-acre corner section in Newark.) Town greens were set aside for drilling the militia or for community grazing of cattle. Newark still has the remains of two such greens—Washington Park and Military Park—ranged along 133-foot-wide Broad Street, a noble width established when the original town was laid out.

The First General Assembly

In the face of such evident local independence, Governor Carteret waited nearly three years before convening New Jersey's first General Assembly. Finally he asked that each of the English towns send two burgesses to Elizabethtown on May 26, 1668. Two burgesses also were allowed the thriving town of Bergen, founded in 1660 and left to prosper under the Dutchmen who had switched allegiance to King Charles. These burgesses were to be joined by two representatives allocated to the far-off "Delaware Settlements."

Despite a heavy Puritan dominance, the first Assembly reflected the divergences of religious and civil opinion within the province. The existence of Baptists in Middletown, Quakers in Shrewsbury, and the Dutch in Bergen allowed some area for polite disagreement in religious matters. The presence of Governor Carteret in Elizabethtown, surrounded by his personal courtiers and servants, served to soften the sharp edge of Puritanism. Congeniality was tinged with wariness in that May of 1668.

The first Assembly was especially concerned with public morals. It enacted a harsh criminal code that reflected Puritan thinking. As in New England, the laws provided death for offenses ranging from burglary to

46

murder and from bearing false witness to being judged a witch. Children over sixteen who attacked or cursed their parents could be executed unless they proved self-defense. Young people on the streets after 9 P.M. faced swift punishment (usually a public whipping), and anyone taking the name of God in vain was to be fined one shilling—half to be paid the informer, half to the town treasury. Convicted burglars were forced to make restitution and on first offense had a letter T (for thief) branded on the hand. A second offense called for the letter B (for burglar) burned on the forehead. There were provisions for stocks, for whipping posts, for public censure. New Jersey would allow no sinning.

A limited sense of intercommunity responsibility was manifested when the Assembly voted an annual provincial tax of five pounds per town. The burgesses adjourned after five days of mild debate and discussion. They agreed to meet annually on November 1, starting the following autumn.

Local Government

Government was left chiefly to each town, based on collective responsibility. All able-bodied men were obliged to work if given "seasonable warnings." That meant laboring on the multipurpose town meeting-house, the first building in every town. It meant building and repairing roads, putting up and mending community fences, fighting fires, tending cattle, and other work that benefited all the town. Work was a form of taxation: the richest were expected to labor the greatest number of days on any project. When ditches were required in Newark's extensive marshes in 1669, a day of digging was asked for each two hundred pounds sterling of individual net worth. A "day's work" was not eight hours; it was completion of a ditch two rods long (thirty-three feet), two feet wide, and two feet deep—no matter how long it might take. If a slacker refused to work "when warned," a substitute was hired and paid by the nonworker.

Every town had two "fence viewers" established by Assembly law and important in a time when lost cattle or hogs were a serious blow.

Towns also had "common branders" charged with branding horses or notching the ears of cattle and hogs with varying "ear marks" to establish ownership. Straying cattle were placed in town enclosures, and owners had to pay a "penny a head" to get them back. Owners of unruly cattle, horses, oxen, or cows found in the town-owned "common field" were fined five shillings per beast plus assessment of all damages. If cows were adjudged "not unruly" (surely a fine point of law), the fine was only four shillings.

Commerce thrived on barter. Taxes were paid and necessities acquired with whatever a man possessed and others needed—corn, wheat, vegetables, milk, butter, nails, or boards. In his first years in Newark, Mr. Pierson was rewarded for his ministerial efforts with a house and a salary in "several kinds of payments," including "a pound of butter for every milk cow in town."

By a provincial law adopted in May, 1668, every town had to "keep an ordinary [inn or tavern] for the entertainment of travellers and strangers." While Puritans frowned on alcoholic beverages, "unless in case of necessity" (as Newark's Town Minutes said), each town had a dispenser of liquors. Jasper Crane, staunchest of Puritans and one of Newark's founders, in 1673 secured "liberty to sell liquors in town." He gladly took wheat in exchange for his beverages.

Young people, not expected to be heard, were expected to be seen when a myriad of chores were to be accomplished. Girls helped in soap- and candlemaking, housecleaning, cooking, and the minding of younger children. Boys worked beside their fathers in roadbuilding and ditchdigging and helped with all other male duties, including chasing wayward cows. Most younger children went to school, usually under the strict tutelage of the town-supported minister, who taught them to read the Bible and to figure simple mathematical problems. Church attendance was mandatory, but Newark's records tell of Puritan boys who "do misbehave themselves" by "sleeping, whispering or the like" in the meetinghouse. Adults were appointed to "see that the boys and youth do

The meetinghouse of colonial times in the typically "New England" towns of northeastern New Jersey was many things. It served as a place of worship, as a schoolhouse, and, in times of danger from Indian attack, as a fortress. Note the guard towers on both sides of the meetinghouse.

carry themselves reverently in the time of public worship on the Lord's Day and other Days."

From Huts to Permanent Settlements

These eastern New Jersey settlers lived their first winter in crude cabins or huts, sometimes nothing more than cave dwellings or lean-tos for shelter against the winter winds. But within five years, most of them lived in fairly comfortable houses. Typical might have been the dwelling of William Meeker, built in 1764 at the south end of Newark. Meeker's low-slung, shingled frame house was much like the saltbox dwellings associated with New England. Inside, a tremendous fireplace provided heat, light, and cooking facilities. The fireplace was at one end of the main room, unlike the New England practice of putting the fireplace more centrally located in the center of the back wall. Every

When the Puritans came from the New England area to Elizabethtown and Newark, they retained the style of architecture that they had known back home. A good example was the famed Meeker House in Newark. Built in 1674, in the southern part of the city, it stood until 1913. This drawing of the Meeker home was made in 1889. It still looked much as it did in its original days.

evening a new log, as much as eight feet long, was placed on the fire, banked with burning embers and allowed to smoulder through the long night.

More than anything, these first settlers were self-centered and independent. Each town saw itself as responsible only unto its own people and to its own strict version of God. Such independent spirit quickly spelled extreme difficulty for Carteret. Rebellion first flamed up in May of 1668 because of the levy of a small provincial tax. All towns hedged on payments, and Monmouth settlers refused outright. The second Assembly, which convened in Elizabethtown on November 1, 1668, boldly protested Carteret's "expectations that things must go according to your opinions." That session ended in complete discord, and seven years elapsed before another Assembly would legally meet.

The Duke of York's carelessness in 1664 now fell heavily on Governor Carteret's shoulders. Settlers in Elizabethtown and Monmouth particularly resented the thought that Lord Berkeley and Sir George Carteret claimed ownership of land that the settlers had acquired through Governor Nicolls, who they had believed was England's official representative in 1664. Philip Carteret's superiors, on the other hand, expected him to collect an annual rent of a halfpenny an acre beginning on March 25, 1670. Amicable enough in 1665, that was intolerable by 1670.

Since Newarkers had acquired their land with Carteret's aid, they decided to honor the commitment on that fateful March 25. Townspeople decided to pay all town rents in a lump sum. They appointed Henry Lyon and Thomas Johnson to "take and receive every man's just share and proportion of wheat for his land." Lyon and Johnson hauled Newark's wheat to Elizabethtown and faced an angry Carteret. He refused to take the "country fare" offered by Newark, demanding gold or silver. Lyon and Johnson took the grain back to Newark.

The People Oppose Philip Carteret

Trouble befell the governor in Elizabethtown. Carteret infuriated the citizens by selling a house lot to one of his servants without town permission. He then stripped two town-appointed militia officers of their commissions. When he gave another house and lot to a servant named Robert Michell, townspeople rioted. They pulled down a log fence around Michell's property, drove hogs through his garden, and ripped clapboards off his house. Carteret pressed charges against two of the fence busters and hog releasers. Dissent soared to the boiling point when the hand-picked panel found the two guilty.

A rebellious, self-appointed Assembly came together in May, 1672, without "the knowledge, approbation or consent" of the governor. They scorned Carteret by electing James Carteret, the dissolute son of Sir George, as the first (and only) "President of New Jersey." Shocked and frightened, the bewildered Philip Carteret promptly booked passage home to report on the mutinous residents of New Jersey. He swore "to cure this wound by speedy medicine which delay may cause to gangrene." Carteret sensed a colonial obstinacy that boded no good for England.

Jerseymen hoped to rid themselves of Philip Carteret and the hateful property rents by peaceful means. They agreed in July, 1673, to join in petitioning the proprietors "for removing of the grievances incumbent." Jasper Crane of Newark, normally a mild Puritan, headed a five-man committee named to consider sending a messenger to England to argue New Jersey's case before the Duke of York and anyone else who would listen.

The Dutch Recapture New York

That messenger never sailed. Before July was out, five Dutch vessels "surrounded" New York and recaptured it in another of the strangely gentle battles that typified Dutch colonial "warfare." The Dutch conquerors renamed New York "New Orange" and demanded loyalty. The Puritans living in New Jersey cared little; in view of their openly

One of the best places to look for evidence of the colonial past is New Jersey's largest city, Newark. Looking south from the Public Library, the outline of the triangular-shaped old Military Green is still visible. Above it towers the steeple of Trinity Episcopal Church, giving a "New England" look to the area. On the right is Broad Street, laid out in 1667 as the broadest street in all of colonial America and today still a wide, graceful avenue in the midst of a teeming city.

hostile attitude toward Charles II and the Stuarts, manifested long before, when many of them lived in Connecticut, a majority may have secretly welcomed the change. A European government simply could not insist on loyalty from people three thousand miles distant and two generations removed in love of the homeland.

Dutch occupation of New York was brief. England regained the territory in the spring of 1674, again without bloodshed, and Philip Carteret returned to New Jersey a year later. He showed such goodwill in his relations with New Jersey landholders that eighty-five Elizabethtowners applied for new land patents between 1675 and 1678. Proprietors agreed to take rents in country pay, particularly grains, but they never relented in their insistence that the rents *must* be paid. The festering wounds were not healed; they were simply out of sight for the time being. They would break open again in time, worse than ever. Carteret had not brought back any "speedy medicine."

The English Towns

Eastern New Jersey became firmly established in Philip Carteret's early years, despite the political bitterness. Slowly, every town grew, and most of them had attracted men with the skills needed for new towns—carpenters, boatbuilders, blacksmiths, weaponmakers, farmers, surveyors, nail makers, and others. The steady growth was proved by a Dutch head-count of adult males rounded up to swear allegiance to Holland after the conquest of 1673. The count indicated that more than one thousand people lived in the six English towns and the one Dutch settlement close to New York.

Finding tangible evidence today of the short but vitally important period in New Jersey's history between 1664 and 1673 is difficult. Newark has since become New Jersey's largest city, built and rebuilt several times in three hundred years, sometimes by design, more often after devastating fires. The original town greens (Military Park and Washington Park) are almost exactly the same in area as they were in colonial times and provide pleasant breathing space for this crowded

city. Statues of famed Newarkers (none of them from colonial times) fill both parks. In recent years Military Park was excavated and a multilayer parking lot built underground. Then the park was restored, and although it is not as it was before, the old militia commons remains as a link with three centuries ago.

One unpleasant colonial legacy of Newark, Elizabethtown, and Jersey City (or any other 300-year-old city) is the tangle of city streets. Newark's Broad Street, said to be the widest thoroughfare in colonial times, remains impressively useful in the twentieth century, but side streets intersect one another at strange angles in reflection of simpler days when speed was no consideration. Modern city drivers are not thankful for colonial streets laid on Indian trails, the natural meanderings of cattle, or the crosscuts of small boys.

Some early town records persist. The Town Minutes of Woodbridge and Newark are preserved at the New Jersey Historical Society. The original lease for New Jersey, the record of the ill-fated gift from the Duke of York to Berkeley and Carteret in 1664, is in the New Jersey Historical Society, as is a copy of the *Concessions and Agreements* brought by Philip Carteret in 1665. Some original Indian deeds can be found, notably the deed that the Elizabethtown Associates obtained from the Indians in October, 1664, now in the New Jersey Historical Society.

Those first English days are difficult to follow except in incomplete

54

"Our town on the Passaic River" as it reportedly looked in 1708. This drawing, for *Leslie's Magazine* in 1866, was made from old plans. On the left is a town tavern and on the right can be seen the village meetinghouse.

archives and in traditions. There are no colonial buildings, few pieces of furniture, few personal effects, no contemporary paintings of the New Jersey of that time. The best visual portrayals are murals painted in 1906 on the walls of the Essex County Court House in Newark. One, by the noted historical illustrator Howard Pyle, recreated from records and traditions the landing of Philip Carteret in Elizabethtown in 1665. The other, painted by muralist C. Y. Turner, depicted the landing of Robert Treat and his Milford followers at Newark.

A portion of the Turner mural perpetuates one of Newark's most enduring early traditions. It shows two young people holding hands on shore in affection. She is seventeen-year-old Elizabeth Swaine; he is her future husband, Josiah Ward. Tradition says that these young lovers were the first settlers to step ashore in Newark. It is a good tradition, for can a city begin better than with love?

CHAPTER THREE

West New Jersey's Quakers

New Jersey's brief return to Dutch rule in 1673 and 1674 provided King Charles II and the Duke of York with ample legal opportunity to reclaim the land if they had so wished, since all previous titles or grants had been voided by the Dutch action. But neither Charles nor the Duke cared for such weighty matters as foreign real estate. Charles reassigned New Jersey to the Duke of York in June, 1674; the Duke, in turn, looked favorably once more to his old friends, Sir George Carteret and John, Lord Berkeley.

Times had changed, much for the worse, the situations of both Berkeley and Carteret. The latter recently had been expelled from the House of Commons for bribery and other dishonest practices. Berkeley had been "detected in the basest corruption" and deprived of public office, and his monetary difficulties were so intense by 1674 that he had to withdraw entirely from contention in both England and New Jersey.

Such scandals had no effect when the Duke of York reaffirmed Carteret's share of New Jersey. But by June, 1673, Berkeley's life had become a mysterious tangle. His reckless disposal of his New Jersey holdings led to a major turning point in American history, however, for it involved William Penn in American affairs for the first time.

The Berkeley-Fenwick Deal

Hoping to retrieve some of his vanished fortune, Berkeley sold his share of the province to John Fenwick in the spring of 1674, "for and in consideration of one thousand pounds." Fenwick, a newly converted Quaker, was a strange candidate for Berkeley's goodwill. He had been a high officer in Oliver Cromwell's forces that had driven the Stuarts from office in the 1640's. If ever there was an enemy eternally detested by the Stuarts and their friends, it was one of Cromwell's officers. But Berkeley did not fret about such things in 1674.

Fenwick's Quaker faith should also have barred him from any consideration. Members of the Society of Friends had been persecuted in England for many years because they shunned church ritualism and refused to swear oaths or bear arms. Their plain speech and simple manners infuriated those who loved the gay palace life and the pomp of the Church of England. That made Berkeley's action all the more surprising.

The Berkeley-Fenwick deal quickly became clouded with doubts and enmeshed in bickering. Fenwick apparently had acted only as an agent for another Quaker, Edward Byllynge, whose financial situation was so wretched that he did not dare to purchase anything under his own name. Among his many creditors was Fenwick, who claimed Byllynge owed him sums exceeding a thousand pounds sterling. Fenwick kept the deed that he had received from Berkeley, believing it to be a proper payment of the debt.

William Penn and the Society of Friends

Byllynge's public protests embarrassed the Society of Friends, since such quarreling between members violated their philosophy of gentle persuasion. The quarrel involved William Penn in February, 1675, when he negotiated the affair along with Gawen Lawrie (who later would become a governor of New Jersey) and Nicholas Lucas, all Quakers. The three ruled that Fenwick could keep only one tenth of the property purchased from Berkeley. The rest would be divided into "Tenths" and sold to encourage Quaker settlement in the western part of New Jersey.

Fenwick protested wildly. He wrote Penn, and although that letter has been lost it is apparent from Penn's reply that Fenwick had vowed revenge. Penn answered that the trustees would "make a public denial of the person that offers violence to the award made." He pleaded: "O John! let truth and the honor of this day prevail." A few days later, Penn wrote to Fenwick:

> O John! I am sorry that a toy, a trifle, should thus rob men of their time, quiet and more profitable employ. . . . Away with vain fancies, I beseech thee, and fall closely to thy business. Thy days speed on, and make the best of what thou hast. Thy grandchildren may be in the other world before the land thou has allotted will be employed.

That spurred Fenwick to hasty action. He advertised in London papers for colonists willing to leave for New Jersey. He had never been there, but he pictured it as a "happy country," where "any people, especially of inferior rank," might acquire so much land "that he may weary himself with walking over his Field of Corn . . . and let his Stock amount to some hundreds." He concluded: "If there be any terrestrial Canaan 'tis surely here, where the Land floweth with Milk and Honey."

The Quakers Sail for Salem

Fenwick's glowing word pictures failed to convince his wife. She refused to sail, but Fenwick's three daughters, Elizabeth, Ann, and Priscilla, all were aboard his ship, the *Griffin*, when it left London in the summer of 1675. Elizabeth and Priscilla were both married, Elizabeth to John Adams and Priscilla to Edward Chamneys. Their children, two girls and a boy in the Adams family, and a boy and a girl in the Chamneys clan, also were aboard the *Griffin*. The third daughter, Ann, met Samuel Hedge on the long sea voyage, and they were married soon after the ship reached West New Jersey. The *Griffin* carried a total of forty-eight people to a new life in Fenwick's "terrestial Canaan."

Fenwick left behind him a tangle of troubles so involved that they would pursue him the rest of his life. His continuing legal battles with other Quakers had so impoverished him that just before sailing he had mortgaged his deed to West New Jersey to fellow Quakers John Eldridge, a tanner, and Edmund Warner, a poultryman. That action, for the paltry sum of £110, ultimately spelled Fenwick's doom.

Fenwick was sore beset. He had disposed of 148,000 West New Jersey acres to fifty people, even before he knew for sure the extent of his American holdings. The Society of Friends spurned him because of his unpleasant behavior. In addition, the Duke of York had dispatched another governor to New York, giving him authority over an area that any ambitious man would interpret as including New Jersey. The new governor, Edmund Andros, was ambitious. Fenwick would learn that, soon enough.

Doubts and fears temporarily disappeared when the *Griffin* reached New Jersey in November, 1675, and sailed up the Delaware River to a point well inland. Feeling fit and happy for the first time in years, Fenwick named the area Salem, from the old Hebrew word *Sholem*, meaning peace. "Salem," uttered by Fenwick, was as much a wishful prayer as an expression of certainty.

Salem's founders moved briskly against the approaching winter. They laid out rough streets and built temporary houses, proceeding as Fenwick negotiated three separate purchases of the land from the Indians. Knowing nothing to the contrary, the settlers accepted Fenwick's pretentious announcement that he was legally the governor of Fenwick's Colony. In fact, Fenwick had no such power.

The Quintipartite Deed

Penn and other English Quaker leaders recognized that lasting occupation of West New Jersey required a clear grant from the Duke of York. Sir George Carteret's rights in the eastern section were clearly accepted as authorized by the Duke, but the Fenwick-Byllynge negotiations with Berkeley had gone unrecognized. After prolonged negotiations, Carteret agreed, on July 1, 1676, with Penn and other Quakers to a division of New Jersey in the so-called Quintipartite Deed. Quintipartite stemmed from the fact that there were five signers: Carteret on the one side and Penn, Byllynge, Lawrie, and Lucas for the Friends. New Jersey legally had become two colonies: East New Jersey and West New Jersey.

The Quintipartite Deed proved the bargaining sagacity of the Quakers. In addition to securing complete recognition of the Penn-Byllynge claim, the deed provided that New Jersey would be split on a line from Little Egg Harbor on the Atlantic coast to the northwestern tip of the state. That shrewd bargain ensured the Quakers' control of all the Delaware River along the western New Jersey boundary.

(It is important to note that the 1676 division line was vague. Eleven years later a Quaker missionary named George Keith—an East New Jersey proprietor—was hired to survey an actual line. He was two-thirds finished before West New Jerseyans discovered that his line was deep into their territory. Keith's survey, they said, had taken away "ye very heart and cream of ye country." The work was stopped at about midpoint. The final division was not set until 1743, when another line was drawn well to the east of Keith's division. Keith's line persists, nevertheless, since the modern boundary between Burlington and Ocean counties is based almost entirely on the 1687 survey. Keith's survey also forms parts of boundaries of four other modern counties.)

Fenwick Goes to Jail

Fenwick exhibited no lessening of his determination to rule what he considered to be his domain. Governor Edmund Andros warned him in the spring of 1676 that he must obey New York laws and restrictions. Where, Andros asked with considerable justice, were the documents to support Fenwick's claims to Salem? Fenwick was stymied: His deed from Berkeley was in London, in the hands of Warner and Eldridge.

Andros sent notice to Fenwick to report to him in New York. When Fenwick refused to obey, Andros ordered him arrested on September

The home of John Fenwick on Fenwick Point in Salem County. This primitive painting is said to have been executed about the time of Fenwick's death.

25, 1676. More than two months later soldiers broke into Fenwick's home. They fired warning shots when he resisted arrest and carried Salem's doughty "governor" off to New York in chains on December 8.

Fenwick defiantly faced a New York jury on January 5, 1777, on a charge that "He hath with force and arms ryoteously and routeously, with other persons, taken possession of large tracts of land on the east side of the river, which same were within the bounds of His Royal Highness' patent from His Majesty . . ." The jury found him guilty, fined him forty pounds, and ordered him to post a security of five hundred pounds to ensure his good behavior.

Fenwick chose to be jailed, and he was still in his cell in August, 1677, when West New Jersey's development entered a vigorous new Quaker phase under Penn's guidance. As Fenwick languished behind bars, a contingent of 230 Quakers bound for West New Jersey arrived in New York aboard the ship *Kent*. They stopped to pay their respects to Andros, in direct admission that Quaker settlers did not yet fully possess the land along the Delaware River.

Andros permitted Fenwick to leave New York aboard the *Kent* for a return trip to Salem. There is no way of knowing Fenwick's thoughts as he watched the *Kent* disappear upstream on the Delaware after dropping him at his home dock, but he must have known that he would not much longer be a power in America. Genuine Quaker strength had come to New Jersey to replace Fenwick's will-o'-the-wisp dreams.

Colonizing West New Jersey

This voyage of the *Kent* was the first step to develop West New Jersey on a plan that divided the area into one hundred parts—ten parts (or one Tenth) reserved for Fenwick. The remaining ninety shares were offered to Quakers. When the *Kent* sailed, forty shares had been sold, and all one hundred were allocated by 1683. Few of the shareholders were wealthy; only twenty-three bought a full share, and only nine bought two or more shares. Several buyers split shares, so that in all there were 120 original landholders. Small businessmen, merchants, and craftsmen were the principal buyers. One hundred of them were English, seventeen were Irish, and three were Scots.

Penn and his associates sought to split West New Jersey into ten large divisions, or Tenths. The first and second of these were located between Pennsauken Creek and what is now Trenton. The third Tenth, comprising modern Gloucester and Camden counties, became known as the Irish Tenth, since this was the area favored by the Irish buyers. Fenwick held the fourth Tenth, and the land east of modern Cumberland County comprised another region. The proprietors thus ran out of land long before they ran out of Tenths.

Generous terms were offered to prospective colonizers. Any person approved by one of the proprietors was granted seventy acres of land for himself, seventy acres for each additional able manservant, and fifty acres for each "weaker servant" or female worker over fourteen years of age. When a servant's customary term of three or four years expired, he would receive from his master, without charge, fifty acres. The proprietors reserved the right to collect a rent of one penny an acre, but few exercised the privilege. They preferred to sell land outright at the going rate of five to ten pounds for one hundred acres.

Two distinct groups were aboard the *Kent* as she sailed up the Delaware River in the August sun, one from Yorkshire and the other from London. For practical reasons they agreed to inhabit jointly a single town for the first year or two. The Quakers left the *Kent* at a Swedish settlement called New Stockholm on Raccoon Creek where friendly Swedes housed the newcomers and acted as interpreters in discussions of land purchases with the Indians. The colony's first death and the first birth occurred while the Quakers were living at New Stockholm in makeshift tents or in Swedish cow sheds. John Kinsey died of exposure; to balance the score, a daughter was born to Robert and Prudence Power.

An advance party went upstream to plot a town, allocating land west of a main street to the Londoners and east to the Yorkshiremen. Winter closed down cruelly as the settlers moved into rude shanties or caves hollowed out in the riverbanks near their new town. Venison and corn supplied by friendly Lenni-Lenape Indians kept them alive until spring. As the sun warmed, permanent houses rose along High Street and the settlers chose a name: Burlington, in memory of an old Yorkshire village.

The "Concessions and Agreements"

Burlington's Quakers brought with them a remarkable document, the *Concessions and Agreements of the Proprietors, Freeholders and Inhabitants of the Province of West Jersey in America.* Edward Byllynge and William Penn had written the document in 1676 to establish an intensely liberal framework of government and civil liberties. The *Concessions* placed a particular emphasis on individual rights. Its writers said eloquently: "We lay a foundation for after ages to understand their liberty as men and Christians, that they may not be brought in bondage but by their consent; for *we put the power in the people.*" (Italics added.)

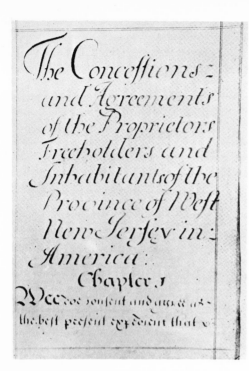

Title page of the *Concessions and Agreements of the Proprietors Freeholders and Inhabitants of the Province of West New Jersey in America.*

The document established a system of secret balloting for an annual election of one hundred assemblymen and ten commissioners of state. Open speech was protected in legislative debate, and citizens could be "witnesses of the votes and inclinations of their representatives." Except for a provision that West New Jersey laws must not conflict with English law, there were no limitations on the powers of self-government in West New Jersey.

The Quaker settlers were assured freedom from illegal arrest or imprisonment for debt, and perjurers were swiftly punished. All persons charged with a crime were granted a trial by jury. Commendably, in a time when most colonizers regarded Indians as "savages" without rights, West New Jersey's laws provided that any Indian charged with a crime must be judged by a jury comprised equally of Indians and settlers. Religious freedom was assured all people: "No man, nor number of men on earth, have power or authority to rule over men's consciences in religious matters." This was not the limited "freedom" of East New Jersey or New England. There were no reservations.

Quakers on the Delaware

Quakers came in large numbers after the *Kent's* safe voyage. More than fourteen hundred Quakers lived in the Burlington and Salem areas in 1681, a year before William Penn founded his City of Brotherly Love on the west bank of the Delaware River. New Jersey's Quakers would look to Philadelphia for leadership; New Jersey's enduring role in the shadow of two great cities had been cast. Interestingly, the quintipartite division of 1676 had delineated the two regions that would revolve around New York and Philadelphia—and Philadelphia was not founded until six years later!

Fenwick continued his posturing in Salem, disturbing even his own loyal settlers and irritating Andros to the point that the New York governor again arrested the impetuous Quaker in 1678 and detained him through the winter. William Penn worked to minimize the power of Andros. Aided by friends in court, Penn was notified in July, 1680, by the Duke of York that West New Jersey residents (including John Fenwick) no longer were responsible to Andros or anyone else in East New Jersey.

Quaker settlements sprang up along the Delaware River or on subsidiary inland streams such as Rancocas Creek or Timber Creek. Often, settlers built their substantial brick homes facing these inland waterways, for the streams were their highways. Today it is easy to find early houses facing a watery "thorofare," even though regular highways or roads run to the rear (now the front) of the houses.

These Quakers who ventured into West New Jersey were men of considerable enterprise, as can be evidenced by Mahlon Stacy. He took his family in a canoe north on the Delaware River to the point where the river surged powerfully over shallow rock formations. Stacy turned that obstacle, "Ye Falles of ye De La Warr," to his advantage by using it to run the first mill in West New Jersey. The village that grew beside Stacy's millsite was called only "Ye Falles" until well after his death in 1704. His son sold eight hundred acres of the Stacy lands in 1714 to William Trent, a wealthy Philadelphia merchant. The place soon became known as Trent's Town, or Trenton, now New Jersey's state capital.

New Jersey's First Banker

The enterprise of another Quaker was quite different. He was Mark Newbie, an Irishman who arrived in Gloucester (in the "Irish Tenth") in 1682, when the West New Jersey Assembly was trying to start a sound money system. Especially needed was a coin of small denomination—and the opportunistic Newbie had brought a large quantity of copper coins. These had been minted in Ireland to honor Saint Patrick, whose likeness appeared on one side of the coin. On the other side was a kneeling king, possibly David. The Assembly recognized that the "Patrick's Pence" could fill its need, and on May 18, 1682, adopted an act that made the Irish pence New Jersey's first official coin. Newbie also became the first official banker. The act read, in part:

> Mark Newbie's half-pence called Patricks half-pence, shall, from and after the said eighteenth instant pass for half-pence current pay of this Province . . . provided that no person or persons be hereby obliged to take more than five shillings in one payment.

Andros and Carteret

Foiled by Penn's deft maneuvering in West New Jersey, Governor Andros turned his attention to East New Jersey. Andros was so puzzled (or so vexed) by Governor Philip Carteret that he journeyed to England in 1678 to seek a ruling from the Duke of York on who really was dominant in East New Jersey. Satisfied in his own mind that East New Jersey properly belonged under his wing, Andros returned to New York in August, 1678, ready to move.

The New York governor sent word to East New Jersey on March 8, 1679, that Carteret could not properly act as governor. Carteret produced his official documents from the Duke of York and cautioned

Andros not to "molest me as governor, nor the people under my charge." Carteret boldly asserted that New Jersey inhabitants would "defend ourselves and our families the best we can." Newark's leaders wrote Andros that they intended to stand solidly behind Carteret unless they received "sufficient order from his Majesty" voiding Carteret's claims.

The Arrest of Philip Carteret

When Philip Carteret's relative and protector, Sir George Carteret, died in England on January 13, 1680, Andros went into action. Andros sailed into Elizabethtown harbor on April 7, 1680, went ashore, and told a throng within the town stockade that he demanded East New Jersey's surrender. When the crowd behaved "somewhat churlishly" (in Andros' words), Carteret led the gathering out into an open field to lessen the tension. During the discussion, Captain John Berry of Newark informed Andros that his actions already were being appealed to England. Andros choked back his fury long enough to join Carteret and their close followers in a lavish banquet.

Immediately upon his return to New York, Andros ordered the arrest of Carteret and dispatched soldiers across the Hudson River to seize the East New Jersey governor. Jasper Danckaerts, a German traveler of the period, related his memory of the incident in a journal of his travels in America:

> They entered the house, I know not how, at midnight, seized him naked, dragged him through the window, struck and kicked him terribly, and even injured him internally. They threw him, all naked as he was, into a canoe, without any cap or hat on his head, and carried him in that condition to New York, where they furnished him clothes and shoes and stockings, and then conducted him to the fort and put him immediately into prison.

Andros was in for a shock, however, when he brought Carteret before a New York jury in May, 1680. Three times Andros demanded that Carteret be found guilty of riot and illegal government. Three times the jury returned "not guilty" verdicts. After the third attempt, the jury told Carteret to return to New Jersey, cautioning him "not to assume any authority or jurisdiction there." Andros took that as support for himself. He met with the East New Jersey Assembly in June, 1680, to tell it he had assumed control.

Chagrined and humiliated, Carteret settled down to hope for vindication. While he waited, Carteret married a Long Island widow, Elizabeth Smith Lawrence, and moved her and her seven children by her previous marriage into his Elizabethtown mansion. His fellow Jerseymen, who had applauded his bravery in facing the New York jurors, did not stretch their sympathies to include cooperation when Philip was restored as governor in October, 1680, by English decree. The East New Jersey Assembly quarreled heatedly with Carteret in October, 1681, in belief that their rights were being eroded. Carteret promptly dissolved the legislature. A year later, in December, 1682, he died. His widow wrote Philip's mother in England that the forty-four-year-old governor's death was hastened by the "barbarious and inhuman action of Sir Edmund Andros and his merciless soldiers."

The Quakers Purchase East New Jersey

The trustees of Sir George Carteret's estate offered East New Jersey at public auction in February, 1682. William Penn and eleven English partners purchased all the province for the bargain price of £3,400. Soon another twelve men, six of them from Scotland, bought into the project, and East New Jersey became the common property of the self-styled "Twenty-Four Proprietors." Twenty of them were Quakers. King Charles endorsed fully the rights of this group in March, 1683.

Thus, for a time, Quaker leaders owned both East and West New Jersey, possibly still envisioning a Quaker territory extending from the Hudson River to Maryland. This was unlikely in view of the vigor with which the Puritan settlers of Newark, Elizabethtown, Middletown, and elsewhere preserved their town rights—against their governor or anyone else. More likely, the Quakers were simply good businessmen. The Quaker dream for New Jersey centered on the settlements along the Delaware.

There the Quakers expanded through the last two decades of the seventeenth century, stamping on the region a lasting individuality. It lingers yet, despite an intense urbanization in a large arc east of Philadelphia. The "Quaker way" is still very much a hallmark. Meetinghouses are prominent in many towns, several of them impressive two-story brick buildings. Quaker-built houses of the late-seventeenth and early-eighteenth centuries are numerous, particularly the unusual "patterned brick" houses of Salem and adjacent counties. These houses show distinctive patterns (diamond shapes, zigzag lines, etc.) as well as dates and initials formed by blue-glazed bricks set among the more usual red bricks.

The liberal traditions and low land prices in West New Jersey encouraged property ownership, accounting for relatively large farm holdings in West New Jersey (known more familiarly today as southern New Jersey or South Jersey). Farms of three hundred and more acres are still common throughout Burlington, Gloucester, Salem,

The Quakers' desire to preserve their religion reached out to encompass a desire for proper education. One of the oldest schoolhouses in the state is the Quaker schoolhouse built in Mount Holly in 1759.

and Cumberland counties, although demands for land are dooming many farms.

Quaker serenity remains to impress visitors in such towns as Burlington, Bordentown, Moorestown, Haddonfield, Woodbury, Salem, Woodstown, and a dozen other places. Old family ties are revered and history seems more alive here than in any other part of the state. Burlington should be recognized as the very foundation stone of American Quakerism, for neither Fenwick's uncertain start in Salem nor Penn's later rise to fame in Philadelphia can erase the fact that Burlington was the place where solid Quaker settlement in this country really began.

Burlington's West New Jersey Proprietors (organized in 1688) have carefully preserved, through nearly three hundred years, the *Concessions and Agreements*. The multipaged, handsomely embossed document is shown occasionally to visitors as an enduring reminder that many of the liberties set forth in the Declaration of Independence or in the later Bill of Rights of the Constitution were available in West New Jersey a full century, and more, earlier.

A hallmark of southern New Jersey is the patterned brick house. One of the oldest, built in 1740, can be seen at Georgetown. The date and initials of the builder are formed by blue-glazed bricks set into the red ones. From an engraving by Earl Horter.

CHAPTER FOUR

Divided New Jersey

When William Penn and the Quakers turned their chief attention to Pennsylvania, leadership in East New Jersey fell into the hands of the Scots among the proprietors. They sought to capitalize on the fact that savage religious persecutions in Scotland would make many Scots eager to escape to a colony in America. So East New Jersey became chiefly a Scottish undertaking for a time. The Scottish proprietors publicized liberally the wonders of the colony in an effort to attract colonists.

Chief among the East New Jersey publicists was George Scot, who was hired in 1685. He had not been to East New Jersey, but he likened the climate to that of sunny Naples. Scottish pulses beat faster at his vivid descriptions of the fishing, the forests, the fertile fields, and the abundance of wild game. In this Garden of Eden, according to Scot, apple trees grown from seed would produce in four years "such a quantity of apples as yielded a barrel of cider." He said that Sandy Hook Bay was not inferior to any harbor in America. What Scot lacked in knowledge he more than made up for by imagination.

Scot knew that East New Jersey desperately needed skilled craftsmen. He wrote that "all Sorts of Tradesmen may make a brave livelyhood there, such as Carpenters, Shipwrights, Rope-makers, Smiths, Brickmakers, Taylors, Tanners, Cowpers, Mill-Wrights, Joyners, Shoe makers and such like." Scot's emphasis on professions proved that his employers were serious about colonization. The days of the gold-seeking adventurer were gone.

The proprietors of East and West New Jersey have been important in the state's development and history for nearly three hundred years. New Jersey was divided in 1676 and until 1702 was two colonies rather than one. The name "The Jerseys" lasted until well after the Revolution. Even today, New Jersey has a decided east and west flavor, revolving around New York and Philadelphia. These are the seals of the two proprietory groups.

The Scots elected one of their number, Robert Barclay, as governor of East New Jersey in September, 1682. He spent much of 1682 and 1683 in Scotland recruiting settlers. At the same time he also sold so many shares in the East New Jersey venture that soon most of the proprietors were Scots. Barclay sent Thomas Rudyard to New Jersey as deputy governor in November, 1682. Rudyard was a noted Quaker and a business associate of William Penn. He brought with him plans for a capital town at Amboy Point, renamed Perth Amboy in honor of the Earl of Perth. It was expected that Perth Amboy would accommodate more than a hundred families.

The Scots

Most of the Scottish settlers who came to New Jersey hoped to improve their desperate lots. Many indentured servants were among them. Three ships brought more than four hundred colonists before the fall of 1684. George Scot was so carried away by his own publicity material that he organized the most ambitious Scottish expedition aboard the ship *Henry and Francis* in September, 1685. Among the more than one hundred persons aboard were several political prisoners who had been released on their promise to leave for New Jersey. Ravaging fever struck the *Henry and Francis* on the high seas, killing more than half the colonists. George Scot and his wife both died at sea. No other Scottish ship was ever sent.

Most of the Scots contentedly settled in Perth Amboy and worked to build a new town. Some moved inland and located as far away as Scotch Plains and Plainfield. They blended readily with earlier settlers, although at first the ambitious newcomers complained about the "laziness" of the people in Elizabethtown, Piscataway, and Woodbridge.

The Scottish proprietors inaugurated a new type of land ownership in East New Jersey by distributing large tracts of land as shareholder dividends. By 1702, three such dividends amounted to 17,500 acres "each" for a full share. Large estates of a thousand or more acres became common along the upper reaches of the Raritan River and in Monmouth County. The upper Raritan became New Jersey's "estate country." Many large estates remain in the hills of Somerset and Morris counties.

To consolidate the records of their extensive land deals, the Scots established the East New Jersey Council of Proprietors in August, 1684. The East New Jersey Proprietors still exist as one of the oldest corporations in America, with headquarters in a little building in Perth Amboy. Its counterpart group in West New Jersey has its own Board of Proprietors, founded in 1688 and housed in a small building in Burlington. The proprietors still meet in Perth Amboy or Burlington in annual revivals of two of America's oldest corporate traditions.

The Pine Barrens

Dependence on water transportation generally kept settlers close to the streams that emptied into the Delaware or Hudson rivers. West New Jersey settlers who pushed eastward from the Delaware River avoided the sprawling pine woodland that covered more than a fourth

73

of New Jersey. The white sand on the forest floor hindered wagon travel even worse than mud. Farmers who shunned the woodland named it the Pine Barrens because they could not imagine farm crops growing there. Actually the area is far from barren; nature lovers since have come to recognize the Pine Barrens as one of the richest botanical treasures in the East. It is still a haven for those seeking such exotic natural treasures as wild orchids or rare ferns.

The long stretch of sandy coastline, now known internationally as the Jersey Shore, was no attraction. Only an occasional squatter dwelled by the sea, fishing, beachcombing, or occasionally rounding up stray cattle that were found wandering along the open beaches. The only exceptions to this casual seaside squatting were the whalers at such places as Long Beach Island and Cape May.

Cape May's whalers were around even before New Jersey was granted to Berkeley and Carteret. They came originally from New England, many of them directly descended from the pilgrims who had arrived on the *Mayflower*. (One noted genealogist has claimed that

Shipwrecks were numerous along the Jersey coast until a system of lighthouses was begun thirty years before the Revolution. This old print shows Sandy Hook Lighthouse, built in 1762. It is still in place and is this country's oldest continuously lighted lighthouse.

74

more descendants of *Mayflower* passengers live in Cape May than any place else except Plymouth.) The Cape May whalers built thirteen houses at Town Bank on a high bluff overlooking the Delaware Bay, and from there they could sight whales—some weighing up to 250 tons. Whaling took a great deal of courage, since the whalers worked from very small boats. The hunts took many lives, but whalers felt the profits were worth the risks. A single whale beached and turned into whale oil could mean one thousand pounds in gold. William Penn wrote of eleven Cape May whales "caught and worked into oyle in one season." Gabriel Thomas wrote in 1698 of three whaling companies at Cape May Point and said "prodigious, nay—vast—quantities of oyle and whalebone" were produced.

The First Counties

Englishmen in New Jersey wanted a legal system to be established between their town courts and the provincial lawmakers. In November, 1675, four counties were formed in East New Jersey: Bergen, Essex, Middlesex, and Monmouth. Boundaries were defined in 1682. Bergen embraced most of what is now Hudson and part of Bergen counties. Essex included both Newark and Elizabeth. Middlesex was not precisely bounded but was far greater than the present county of that name. Monmouth comprised the present counties of Monmouth and Ocean.

Settlers in the Raritan River valley caused the East New Jersey Assembly to split away a portion of Middlesex on May 14, 1688, to establish Somerset County. The reason given was unusual: "The uppermost part of the Raritan River is settled by persons, who, in their husbandary and manuring their lands, are forced upon quite different ways and methods from other farmers and inhabitants of Middlesex county . . ."

East New Jersey's counties brought together towns to share the courts, and people were oriented to their towns. West New Jersey's county system was based on social and economic considerations, where people associated themselves politically with a county shire town (county seat). West New Jersey counties stemmed from the Tenths that the Quakers originally used to divide the area. The first and second Tenths—the Yorkshire and London Tenths—became Burlington County. The third and fourth Tenths were made into Gloucester County, and the fifth and sixth Tenths became Salem County. The Cape May area became a county in November, 1692. All of these West New Jersey counties were much larger than counties of the same name are today. The original county of Burlington, for example, included all of modern Burlington County as well as all of Hunterdon, Morris, Sussex, and Warren counties.

Six of the counties—Monmouth, Essex, Somerset, Burlington, and Gloucester—all were named in sentimental remembrance of homelands in England. Bergen County honored the town founded in 1660 by the Dutch. Cape May was named for the Dutch navigator Cornelius Mey, and Salem stemmed from the old Hebrew word for peace.

The Young Move West

County boundaries were of little consequence to the slowly increasing numbers of people who came to New Jersey as the seventeenth century began to wane. Dutch settlers and their large families moved outward from the banks of the Hudson River, keeping their Dutch traditions as well as their Dutch ways with the land. It was reported that on Bergen Neck (Bayonne), Dutchmen raised cabbages so big they were called "governor's head" and fishermen hauled in oysters so large they were called "governor's foot." Curiously, since the Hackensack River valley in time became New Jersey's chief Dutch stronghold, the first permanent settler there was David Des Marest, a French Huguenot who objected to helping support the Dutch Reformed Church in New York. He led his family up the Hackensack River in 1677 to take over about five thousand acres of land at what is now New Milford.

Before 1700, second generations of young people in Newark and

Elizabethtown began a westward movement that would lead across the highlands of New Jersey and eventually across the Delaware River and on to the open western lands beyond the Allegheny Mountains. For Newark's young people "the west" meant the land that town leaders had bought in March, 1678, to extend Newark's boundaries to the top of the Orange Mountains. That purchase from the Indians of about seven square miles cost "two guns, three coats, and thirteen cans of rum." A future for new families lay on the gentle slopes. Cattle grazed there could supply both meat and hides. Rapid streams on the hills could power mills to saw wood and grind grain. The movement to the mountaintops was slow, for the thick woodland had so many wolves and bears that bounties for killing them were offered by Newark as late as 1702.

Young people moving westward from Elizabethtown traveled south of the rugged Watchung Mountains to find easily tilled soil. Colonists established Connecticut Farms (now Union) in 1667. In 1684, Scottish families from Perth Amboy came overland and founded Scotch Plains and Plainfield. Towns were easily named, usually after geographic prominences or the first settlers. A good illustration is recorded about Elizabethtown in 1699, when settlers divided the pasturelands well to the west of their town—and simply called their place Westfield.

Settlements Grow

The wide Raritan River both helped and hindered colonization. It easily led settlers to the rich uplands, but the river's width also hindered east-and-west travel. Those journeying between New York and Philadelphia at first forded the river only at rocky shallows. Then, in 1686, John Inian established a ferry as the first exploitation of Middlesex County's position astride roads between east and west. Inian's ferry attracted other settlers, and in 1730 the place was renamed New Brunswick in honor of the House of Brunswick, then occupying the throne of England.

Monmouth County, wealthiest in the province in the 1680's, was known as "a great resort for industrious and reputable farmers." Despite that reputation its growth was slow. A boatload of stranded Scotsmen worked inland from the coast in 1685 to found Freehold. Some Dutchmen from New York took up land in the 1690's, and French Huguenots settled in the county before 1700. Nearly all activity in the county continued to center on the original towns of Middletown and Shrewsbury.

There was movement also in West New Jersey. Thomas Farnsworth went eight miles up the Delaware River from Burlington in 1682 to found Farnsworth's Landing (now Bordentown) on a high bluff overlooking the Delaware River. John Wills, son of Burlington's first physician, started a famous gristmill on Rancocas Creek in the 1690's and attracted customers all the way from Little Egg Harbor on the Atlantic Ocean.

Salem County was prominent by the time John Fenwick died in November, 1683, after living long enough to see his town on Salem Creek made an official port of entry in 1682. One of Fenwick's dreams had been a town called Cohansey, to be built on Cohansey Creek along a street one hundred feet wide and two miles long. A year after Fenwick's death, Quakers from Salem and Presbyterians and Baptists from New England bought sixteen-acre plots besides "Ye Greate Streete" in Greenwich, their name for Cohansey. Greenwich was made a port of entry in 1687 as proof of the brisk trade that crossed its docks. Much later, in 1774, little Greenwich had a memorable brush with destiny that will be told in a later chapter.

Cape May needed more than whalers for genuine settlement. Specifically, it needed relief from the tight land control of Dr. Daniel Coxe of London. Dr. Coxe had purchased, sight unseen, ninety thousand Cape May acres in 1688 and had ordered that a fine structure, named Coxe Hall, be built in the whaling village. The two-story hall was used for Quaker and Baptist church services as well as for the first courts convened after Cape May County officially was established in 1692. Many families came there to live—people named Hand, Leaming,

Townsend, Spicer, Schellenger, Hughes, and Ludlam. All of those family names are traceable to the 1690's; all of them still are familiar in Cape May County.

Settlement of West New Jersey generally was from the Delaware River eastward, but three important exceptions occurred in what is now Mercer County. Three brothers, Jonathan, James, and David Stout, of the big and notable Monmouth County Stout family, came westward in 1686 on a hunting trip in the Hopewell Valley. The area so charmed them that they soon deserted their sandy shore to live permanently at Hopewell. Eight years later, in 1694, Ralph Hunt and Theophilous Phillips of Long Island bought land at Maidenhead (today's Lawrenceville). Modern Princeton was settled in 1695 by Long Island Quakers headed by John Stockton. He was the forerunner of the illustrious Stockton family, whose name echoed throughout much of early American history.

This picture shows the simple way of making leather in colonial New Jersey, an important industry in the Elizabethtown and Newark areas.

First Industry

Colonists needed to be self-sufficient. Each farmer grew all his own crops, raised his own apples for cider, grazed and milked his own cattle, and slaughtered his own hogs and steers for beef. His wife made clothing for the entire family, first spinning sheared wool into homespun cloth. Mothers and daughters made candles and soap. The few luxuries or necessities that could not be made were imported from England. But slowly industry was beginning—in such places as Newark and Elizabethtown, near to the New York markets, and in Monmouth County, where bog iron in the river bottoms led to the colony's first iron industry.

John Ogden of Elizabethtown, New Jersey's first leather maker, began as early as 1664. Ogden's village became known as the "Mother of tanners," sending trained leathermen throughout the Middle Atlantic provinces. Newark invited one Samuel Whitehead of Elizabethtown to come over in 1680 to "inhabit among us, provided he will supply the town with shoes." Newark warned Whitehead that "for the present we know not of any piece of land convenient." Despite that halfhearted invitation, historians believe that Whitehead accepted the offer. Several tanners congregated by Newark's "water place" before 1700, close to the good water bubbling down from cool springs on the slopes west of town.

New Englanders began New Jersey's iron story in 1674, when James Grover of Shrewsbury decided to build an iron forge beside his gristmill. He invited the celebrated ironmaking Leonard brothers down from Lynn, Massachusetts, and they supervised construction of the first ironworks in the colonies outside of New England. Colonel Lewis Morris, a wealthy merchant from Barbados, acquired Grover's works in 1676, but the enterprise was never successful. Nearly a century passed before ironmen turned seriously to the bog iron that was so rich in southern New Jersey streams.

Waterpower was of vital importance to offset the scarcity of manpower. The rapidly flowing rivers of northern New Jersey provided natural velocity, but sluggish streams in the lowlands had to be dammed to create power. Windmills often were used close to sea level; there are records of windmills at Bergen and Newark in East New Jersey and on Windmill Island in the Delaware River between Camden and Philadelphia. Water-powered or wind-driven mills replaced the housewives and older daughters who in early days had made flour by grinding grain by hand. Newark sought a miller in 1668 to "grind all the town's grist into good meal." Woodbridge's miller was required to furnish "two good stones of at least five feet across." He received in return a land grant and one sixteenth of all the grain that he ground.

Early Trading

Jerseymen also sought trade with the outside world. Perth Amboy's founders believed that their port could provide an alternative to New York's busy docks, but the hope was never realized. Burlington reported in the late part of the seventeenth century that it had "a commodious dock for vessels, many fine wharves and large timber-yards, malt houses, brew houses, bake houses. They produce bread, beer, beef and pork, butter and cheese, with which they freight several vessels and send them to the Barbadoes and other Islands." Salem at the same time boasted that it exported "deerskins, cedar posts, shingles, and bolts, staves, wheat, corn, sunbeef, pork and tallow, sent chiefly to New York, Boston and the West Indies." It is probable that both Burlington and Salem indulged in more than a little provincial boasting.

In truth, there was little interchange even between East and West New Jersey, much less with the world. Travelers between the provinces followed an old road laid out by the Dutch to connect New Amsterdam and its outposts along the Delaware River. The road ran from Elizabethtown to the Raritan River, where horses and men alike splashed across a shallow ford at what is now New Brunswick. Once across, the traveler had two choices. He might take the "Upper Road" to the Delaware at a point where Trenton is now located; or he might traverse the "Lower Road" that branched off five or six miles south of the Raritan and arrive at the Delaware near the present Burlington. Both "roads" were little more than widened foot paths. Even as late as 1716, when a ferry had been established at New Brunswick for twenty years, the rates allowed only for "horse and man" or a "single person."

The East New Jersey proprietors recognized the great need for a good road to link East and West. They instructed Deputy Governor Gawen Lawrie in 1683 to determine "whether there may not a convenient road be found betwixt Perth Town and Burlington, for the entertaining of a land conveyance that way." Lawrie built the new road within a year, connecting it with a ferry between Amboy and New York. Earnest efforts to attract travelers to Lawrie's Road did not swing much traffic from the old Dutch road. The Assembly was asked in 1698 to endorse the Lawrie route. It refused, chiefly because the Assembly three years before had agreed to maintain the older route.

Elsewhere local government cooperated to build roads between emerging towns. A major West New Jersey road from the Falls of the Delaware (Trenton) passed through Crosswicks, Burlington, and on to Salem. Later it was extended to Cohansey Bridge (Bridgetown). Portions of this "Kings Highway" still are known by that name. Haddonfield's chief street, for example, is Kings Highway.

Dissatisfaction and Dissension

Although there was no easy way for settlers to exchange opinions, dissatisfaction was swelling within both New Jersey provinces against rule by the proprietors. Governor Lawrie complained in 1686 of "foul mouth slanders that proceed from murderous spirits in the dark behind my back, who dare not appear to justify me before my face." His troubles were traceable to the old demand by proprietors for annual rents. Second- and third-generation descendants of the first English settlers continued to base land ownership on grants from Governor Nicolls in 1664 or to property purchased from the Indians. Trouble that brewed incessantly through the last four decades of the seventeenth century was near the boiling point in East New Jersey.

West New Jersey's Quakers were not obsessed with rent problems, but in 1684 and 1685 the area's residents elected their own governor in open defiance of Edward Byllynge, who had claimed the sole right to name the governor. Dissension stemmed from the fact that Byllynge argued that the liberal *Concessions and Agreements* of 1676 were no longer valid. When Dr. Daniel Coxe assumed the governorship in 1687 (without leaving England), he agreed with Byllynge. Coxe was not a Quaker, a circumstance not likely to set well, but he promised certain fundamental rights, such as liberty of conscience, trial by jury, and Assembly powers "consistent with the ends of good government." West Jerseyans were mollified for a time.

The Rebellion of 1700

Dissatisfaction exploded into solid rebellion in 1700, with violence so widespread that the disruptions were called "the Revolution." This revolution was not aimed directly at royal government in England, but it was powerful evidence that New Jerseyans insisted on interpreting any authority in the light of how it restricted their personal liberties. Independent thought was maturing in America.

Governor Andrew Hamilton, who had been governor of both East and West New Jersey at various times since 1692, returned from England in 1700 to find all of New Jersey seething with dissent. About 250 East New Jersey leaders sent a petition to King William, repudiating Governor Hamilton. They asked for a governor who could serve as "an indifferent judge" in the growing controversy "between the proprietors and the inhabitants of Your Majesty's Province." Such peaceful protest failed to satisfy many. Mob rule flamed in several areas.

Revolutionists nailed shut the door on the Middlesex County court-house on March 4, 1700, and warned agents of the proprietors to stay off the "property of the people." A week later a court session in Essex County was adjourned after riotous action that an eyewitness wrote "seemed rather to look like a rebellion than otherwise." In mid-July, howling citizens halted a court session in Middletown. The revolution reached its peak between the fall of 1700 and the spring of 1701.

On September 10, 1700, rioters crowded into the Essex County Court to shout approvingly when Samuel Carter of Elizabethtown asked the judges by what authority they sat. The answer, "by the King's," touched off gales of laughter, followed by angry words. When the judges ordered one Samuel Burwell arrested on the charge of not supporting his child, Carter and others attacked the constable, "pulled the chief judge off his bench, beat him with fists and sticks, and broke his sword." The unruly throng ripped clothing off other justices and turned the courtroom into a shambles. Two days later a gang of sixty horsemen rode to the home of Justice Theophilous Pierson in Newark and demanded that he surrender the jail keys. Pierson asked them where they had gotten their power. Samuel Whitehead of Elizabethtown raised his club and yelled, "By this power!" The mob forced the sheriff from a nearby house, took his keys, and freed a political prisoner.

At about the same time, a Monmouth County mob "beate the saide pretended sheriff to the shedding of blood on boath sides" during a jailbreak that freed Richard Salter. Governor Hamilton hastened to the scene with nearly fifty armed men but retreated before a force four times as large. Hamilton faced another crisis in March, 1701, when he ordered a trial at Middletown for Moses Butterworth, one of Captain Kidd's pirates. Townspeople showed their anger by setting militia training for the opening day of the trial. The throb of a "Drum Beating Continually" so disrupted the court that it could not examine Butterworth. Suddenly more than one hundred Middletown militiamen and their friends burst into the courtroom and "did traytorously seize ye Governor and ye Justices, the King's Attorney General and ye under Sheriff, and ye Clerke of ye Court and kept them close prisoners under a guard from Tuesday ye 25 March until ye Saturday following." All of them—governor, justices, court clerks—were held pending recovery of a wounded rioter. It was clearly implied that some high-ranking officials would be executed if the wounded man should die. He recovered. The officials were set free.

West New Jerseyans also rebelled in considerably more restrained fashion than their compatriots in East New Jersey. When Quaker proprietors voted a heavy tax for use in defending proprietary titles, some sixty to seventy angry persons swept into Burlington in March, 1701, in what was described as a "Tumultuary and Riotous manner." They broke open the town jail and temporarily forced the administration into hiding.

England wearied of New Jersey's governmental troubles under proprietary rule. The proprietors decided to yield their powers of governing, fully aware that controlling real estate rather than people would benefit them most. Late in 1701 the Board of Trade in England recommended to the Crown that the provinces of East New Jersey and West New Jersey be united and placed directly under royal rule. The reigns of New Jersey government passed to Queen Anne in 1702; after thirty-eight years of trouble and dissension, New Jersey was a single colony.

CHAPTER FIVE

United New Jersey

L ewis Morris of Monmouth County represented the East New Jersey proprietors in England during the "surrender" of New Jersey to Queen Anne. He insisted above all that the proprietors continue their right to collect rents. The proprietors also asked to choose the first governor of a united New Jersey, hoping that the Queen would approve Andrew Hamilton, a governor of New Jersey at varied times during the troubled 1690's. Hamilton, the proprietors said, was an objective, unbiased man who was unpopular "only with the lawbreakers."

Morris suggested to the Queen that only those "of ye best estate" be appointed to the council that would serve with the governor. In addition, the proprietors urged that high property qualifications be maintained for members of the Assembly. If this was not done, the proprietors explained righteously, "ye Proprietors interest would be at ye disposal of ye tag, rag, and rascality."

The East New Jersey proprietors approved of Morris' actions on their behalf so heartily that they rewarded him handsomely in December, 1702. Since the terms that Morris had gained were "to the general satisfaction of the board," he was granted a new patent for his extensive land holdings in Monmouth County, with a rent of only one pint of spring water per year! His back debts all were canceled, and he was granted a lease for twenty-one years on an enormous acreage extending from the Shrewsburg River to the Manasquan River. The lease gave him the privileges of cutting timber and of manufacturing pitch, rosin, tar, or turpentine. The star of Lewis Morris was on the

Early eighteenth-century dress.

rise. His name would be one to reckon with in the next four decades of New Jersey history.

Queen Anne's Choice for Governor

The surrender did not meet with unanimous approval, however, even among proprietors. William Penn protested that "the surrender was knavishly contrived to betray the people"; a reflection of the fact that West New Jerseyans had not been as actively opposed to the proprietors as people in the eastern province. West New Jersey Quakers also feared that their individual liberties might not be fully protected under a royal government. Thus divisions of opinion would continue to plague whomever Queen Anne chose to be New Jersey's first royal governor. Sadly her choice was quite possibly the worst that could have been made. He was Edward Hyde, better known as Lord Cornbury.

Governor Cornbury had little to recommend him for high position except the fact that he was Queen Anne's cousin. He was described as a man of little intellect, a spendthrift and a bigot. Cornbury's chief hope was that he might quickly ease his money worries in New Jersey.

Cornbury was appointed to rule both New Jersey and New York, disappointing Lewis Morris and others who dreamed that New Jersey might get its own governor. West New Jersey residents were fearful that they might never see Cornbury; they were aware that a governor of these two colonies most certainly would live in New York. Residence there would not help him to understand the particular needs of those who lived far away by the Delaware River.

Queen Anne's governor arrived in August of 1703 and, as expected, settled down in New York while New Jersey's fifteen thousand inhabitants awaited his first call. The queen left little to chance in her instructions to her "captain general and governor in chief of our province of New Jersey." Cornbury brought with him a detailed list of 103 provisions that the Queen expected him to enforce. These included the granting of religious freedom "except for Roman Catholics" and specific means of accomplishing good relationships with the Council and the Assembly. She also suggested methods of dealing with pirates, listed provisions for export and import trade, and stipulated requirements for issuing currency. Queen Anne tried to make the transfer from proprietary to royal government as painless as possible. She insisted that no judges, justices, sheriffs, or other officers be removed "without good and sufficient cause to be signified unto us." Quakers were permitted merely to affirm their loyalty rather than taking an oath against their principles. One of the most peculiar provisions in the list of instructions reflected a continuing fear that New Jersey might again be wracked by discord. The Queen wrote:

> For as much as great inconveniences may arise, by the liberty of printing in our said province, you are to provide by all necessary orders, that no person keep any press for printing, nor that any book, pamphlet or other matters whatsoever be printed without your especial leave and license first obtained.

The restriction prevented New Jersey people from getting their first official newspaper until the American Revolution was under way in 1776. This lack of printed materials is the chief stumbling block to researching New Jersey's colonial history. Since New Jersey depended upon occasional notices in either the Philadelphia or New York newspapers, the "news" could not be expected to be either fresh or unbiased. Reliance on out-of-province newspapers also furthered New Jersey's growing awareness that it was merely a split area annoyingly lodged between America's two greatest towns.

The "Cornbury Ring"

Lord Cornbury's administration quickly deteriorated into unscrupulous pursuit of financial gain. He first supported an alliance of East New Jersey Scots proprietors and West New Jersey Quakers. When those groups refused to give him what he considered an adequate advance salary, he switched his affections to a combination of East New Jersey English proprietors and the West New Jersey Anglican Church faction. His dealings with this latter alliance were to outrage the New Jersey colonists, who derisively termed the partnership the "Cornbury Ring."

The governor and his ring moved boldly, recognizing that a rapid turnover of land would bring the greatest profits in the least time. They seized the offices of the registrar and surveyor general of the East New Jersey proprietors, then diminished Quaker authority in West New Jersey on the grounds that Quakers could not swear an oath of allegiance. The latter action directly defied Queen Anne's instruction that Quakers need not swear an oath. Cornbury's high-riding ring dumped more than a half million acres of New Jersey land on the market between 1706 and 1709.

The Assembly Presents Its Grievances

Voters elected a protesting Assembly in 1707. Cornbury appeared in Burlington to face this new group of New Jersey representatives. After hearing Cornbury's traditional opening address, the Assembly named a committee to consider grievances against the governor. The committee drew up fifteen complaints that they directed Speaker Samuel Jenings to read personally to the governor. The tone was set in the first sentence: "We are obliged to lay before him (the governor) the unhappy circumstances of this province."

The petition complained that Cornbury's long absences from New Jersey made him unaware of local problems. Several of the grievances were minor—including a request that county offices be established for the filing of wills—but the serious charge was levied that Cornbury had acted in a manner "directly repugnant to the Magna Charta, and contrary to the Queen's express instructions." The assemblymen declared flatly that they believed "considerable sums of money" had been given the governor to dissolve the first Assembly. This 1707 document ended with these words: "Liberty is too valuable a thing to be easily parted with." That sentiment would be echoed in all American colonies sixty-five years later.

It was recorded that as Jenings boldly read the list of grievances, Cornbury constantly interrupted with such declarations as "Stop! What's that?" One witness said Jening's behavior was "so odious an insult, so detestable a pride as has never before been offered to the person of a governor." Cornbury remained in the chamber after Jenings had left, turned to those with him, and said with strong feeling that "Jenings had impudence enough to face the Devil!" Robert Quarry, surveyor general of customs, wrote to England that the assemblymen would not be satisfied "unless the Queen will allow them to send representatives to sit in the Parliament of Great Britain!"

Cornbury Is Recalled

Cornbury answered the Assembly charges, denying that he failed to give New Jersey proper attention. However, the Assembly's written grievances on top of many other complaints turned Queen Anne sour on her fortune-hunting cousin. The Queen's patience finally ran out in 1708, when she was quoted as saying that she would not support her "near relations . . . in oppressing her subjects." When Cornbury's New York creditors heard he had lost his power, they had him jailed by the sheriff. He remained there until, on his father's death, he became the Earl of Clarendon and returned to England. It was said that New Jersey (and New York) never had a governor "so universally detested, nor any who so richly deserved the public abhorrence; in spite of his noble descent, his behavior was trifling, mean and extravagant."

Two lackluster successors to Cornbury between 1708 and 1710 gave the Assembly the chance to enact a liberalized voting law that gave the franchise to anyone "worth £50 current money of the province in real and personal estate" (compared with the previous restriction limiting voting only to those with more than one hundred acres of land). The Assembly also came to recognize that their greatest power lay in controlling the governor's wages. This would be a powerful bargaining point with all New Jersey's governors until the time of the Revolution.

Robert Hunter

Governor Robert Hunter arrived in 1710 in the midst of turmoil. Cornbury's Ring still sold land as it pleased, and disagreements between the Assembly and the Council had brought government nearly to a standstill. Hunter won applause from the Assembly in the spring of 1711 by asking the English government to dismiss four members of the powerful Council despite their connections in England. When the Council dismissals were approved, Hunter held a strong position. He pushed through reforms, including reaffirmation of Quaker rights to hold office and to serve on juries without taking oaths. Lowered legal costs opened the courts to broader groups of people. In 1717 the Assembly issued four thousand pounds sterling in paper money, important because later assemblies would be persistently outraged when England failed to sanction paper money in New Jersey.

Hunter liked New Jersey so much and felt so well accepted that he talked of spending his last years in a house that he had built in the province. He has been called "the most nearly ideal governor New Jersey ever had; he was able, talented, eminently respected, and on the whole, popular." When inhabitants of a large area—including all of modern Hunterdon, Morris, Sussex, and Warren counties, and part of Mercer—split from Burlington County in 1714 to form New Jersey's tenth county and the first of the eighteenth century, they honored the popular governor with the county name of Hunterdon. Hunter returned to England with "a violent pain in my hipp," never to live out his dream of retirement in New Jersey.

William Burnet

New Jersey was lucky in Governor Hunter's successor. He was William Burnet, thirty-two years old when he became governor of New York and New Jersey in 1720. He was an impulsive man; he said of himself: "I act first and think afterwards." Despite that low self-esteem, he became one of New Jersey's best governors, a generous and highly sociable man. Burnet quarreled at first with the Assembly, seeking to raise property-holding qualifications for assemblymen and asking for personal financial support for five years. He did not get the increased Assembly qualifications and settled for two years of financial support. After that he normally let the Assembly have its own way. Pleasant relations continued for most of Burnet's regime.

One of Burnet's most important actions was the establishment in 1723 of a New Jersey loan office to increase the amount of paper money in the colony. New Jersey badly needed such currency to combat wildly fluctuating cycles of inflation and deflation that beset this agricultural colony set between New York and Philadelphia. The loan office issued forty thousand pounds of paper money in small bills, the first four thousand to be used to pay state debts. The rest was loaned in amounts up to a hundred pounds secured by mortgages. The enterprise succeeded so well that within two years New Jersey's paper money was considered more valuable than either New York or Pennsylvania currency.

The People Are Restless

Burnet was transferred to Massachusetts in 1727 despite his vigorous protests. By then his popularity was wearing thin; assemblymen noted sarcastically that he had not been in the state for more than two years except for brief visits. Even the friendly rule of Governors Hunter and Burnet could not eclipse the fact that New Jersey ran second in the thoughts of a governor charged with ruling both New York and New Jersey.

Uneasiness stirred within New Jersey. Both Hunter and Burnet wrote home to warn of a rising tide of independent thought. Hunter declared that "ye colonies were infants sucking their mother's breasts, but . . . would wean themselves when they came of age." In 1721, when the New Jersey Assembly protested Burnet's "intermeddling with the business of the house," he dissolved the group by saying it was "evident you are not so much contending with me . . . as directly with his Majesty, whose instructions you have entirely disregarded."

Lewis Morris

New Jersey's hopes for its own governor quickened in the decade after Burnet's departure. John Kinsey, a prosperous, energetic West New Jersey Quaker, and Lewis Morris, who had helped engineer the capitulation of the East New Jersey proprietors to Queen Anne, both asked England for a separate New Jersey governor. The need became even more clear after 1732, when Governor William Cosby arrived. He promised to spend half his time in New Jersey but met with the Assembly only once in the next four years. Provincial government came nearly to a standstill. When Morris sailed for England in 1734 to protest, Cosby was so incensed that he dispatched soldiers to stop the expedition. Morris boarded a vessel near Shrewsbury under a convoy of armed boats from that town and made his way to England.

Begging, pleading, and demanding, Morris spent more than a year in England, setting forth the case for an independent New Jersey. Many ears listened, but no one acted in Morris's behalf. He wrote that he did not believe any Englishmen would risk their reputations "for any such trifle as a plantation governor or all of them put together." A paragraph in a letter from Morris to James Alexander expanded the point:

> We have a Parliament and ministry, some of whom I am apt to believe know that there are plantations and governors, but not as well as we do. Like the frogs of the fable, the pranks of a plantation governor are sport to them though death to us, and they seem less concerned in our contest than we are in those between crows and kingbirds.

Morris wore out his welcome. The Duke of Newcastle, who was responsible for Cosby's position in the new world, asked an intimate what it would take to silence Morris. He was told: "I have reason to believe from himself that if your Grace would please to recommend him to be governor of New Jersey, it would make him easy." Newcastle offered the post to Morris, who refused because he doubted whether the Duke's word was worth much. Cosby died of tuberculosis on March 10, 1736; soon after, Morris left England. With a typical lack of diplomacy he called London, as he departed, "that noisy, stinking and very expensive town."

New Jersey's Own Governor

Morris arrived back home in October, 1736, and proclaimed himself acting governor, only to find that John Hamilton, son of the man who had governed the province in the 1690's, had been appointed to that temporary post. Disappointment followed disappointment for Morris. In June of 1737, Lord Delaware was named governor of New York and New Jersey; it seemed as if the old system of a shared governor would persist. Lord Delaware never left England. He resigned as governor in September to accept appointment as a colonel of the first troop of Life Guardsmen—proof positive of the low regard in which an American governorship was held. England stopped thwarting Lewis Morris: in January, 1738, he was appointed the first governor assigned solely to New Jersey. When news of the appointment reached the colony, it was hailed "to the great satisfaction of the people throughout the provinces."

Morris should have been a popular governor. He had served New Jersey with distinction for nearly a half century and had spoken out often against tyrannical governors. His friends numbered the most influential people in New Jersey and New York, and he displayed an ability to get on well with people of all stations of life. He announced that he would not sit with the Council while it acted in a legislative capacity, a concession that would have given the upper house more independence. The Assembly had not met in five years, and no popular election had been held for eight years. Morris promptly called an election, and the eleventh Assembly convened at Perth Amboy in the autumn of 1738. In his welcoming speech the governor urged assemblymen not to decrease the income of a state official, "thereby laying him under the temptation of taking unbecoming methods of supporting himself." Goodwill was so high in 1739, when the northern section of Hunterdon County broke away to form a new county, that the inhabitants called their new county Morris and their new county seat Morristown, after the then-popular governor.

But Morris soon quarreled with the Assembly over his pay, the leash that long had restrained New Jersey governors. At first Morris won sympathy by reciting how he had secured New Jersey people a governor of their own "at no small expense" to himself. The Assembly rewarded him with five hundred pounds for that, plus a salary of a thousand pounds a year and an allowance of sixty pounds for house rent. Their generous impulses were stilled when Morris sneered that he would accept these sums only as a "down payment" on what he was due. Several assemblymen replied sarcastically that their affection prevented them from giving more, for fear of tempting "someone with great influence at court to seek his governorship." A weaver sitting in the Assembly bluntly said, "Let us keep the dogs poor and we'll make them do what we please." Morris knew exactly what he meant.

Government came again almost to a standstill in the early 1740's. The Assembly insisted on keeping its privileges, especially the right to enact money laws. Morris, in turn, wrote letters constantly criticizing the legislators. Both the governor and his opponents sought as much publicity as possible in the New York and Philadelphia newspapers, since New Jersey still had no newspaper of its own. Wrangling reached a peak when the Assembly met early in 1745. Morris scolded the body for its lack of cooperation, then referred to them as a group of "idiots." The assemblymen said that they would confess to being "farmers and plowmen," but wrote Morris that they vigorously resented being called "idiots."

The Land Question

Suddenly the land difficulties that had plagued nearly every governor since 1664 reappeared to compound the troubles. Expectations that the land riots of the seventeenth century would be ended by ceding the rights of government to the crown were dashed. Since Lewis Morris was one of the architects of that surrender of government, it was supreme irony that he should be a victim when dissension once again struck New Jersey in 1745.

Trouble had been brewing quietly over the unresolved question: Who truly owned the land—the proprietors, the Elizabethtown Associates, the Indians, or the people who directly worked and improved the acres regardless of title? Proprietors charged that anyone who refused to pay the annual rents was a squatter. The proprietors had the law on their side, but those who tilled the acres had the equally potent power of possession.

There were squatters aplenty. A survey in 1735 showed ninety-eight families had occupied thirteen thousand acres of land in Hunterdon County without securing titles from the proprietors. The survey probably understated the case, since squatters threatened to kill agents of the proprietors if they dared to enter the area. Hoping to get legal proof of improper use of land, three leading proprietors—James Alexander,

Robert Morris, and David Ogden—began a search in the "Horseneck" section of western Essex County. That area today includes the Caldwells, Roseland, and Livingston. The fact that Robert Morris was the son of the governor was not likely to appease the settlers.

The Horseneck settlers claimed they had purchased the land directly from the Indians in 1702. However, when the proprietors asked to see the deed, it was said that by a curious coincidence it had been lost when the house of John Pierson burned down. Alexander, Morris, and Ogden

Map drawn in 1747 for the *Bill in the Chancery* suit offers an excellent view of northeastern New Jersey. It shows, among other things, the road that extended from Elizabethtown to the Delaware River (called the Zuidt River, after the old Dutch name). It also shows how scattered were the towns. The old Indian path that the Indians followed across the province from the Delaware River to the ocean is shown as the Minisink Path, or the Indian Path from Navesink to Minisink.

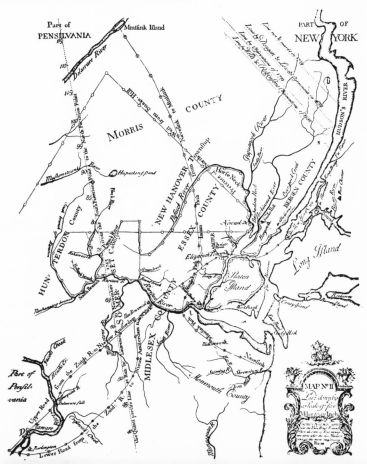

filed in court an action called the Bill in Chancery, wherein sixty people among the Elizabethtown Associates were identified as holding land improperly. The judge trying the case would be Governor Morris himself, who was so in favor of the proprietary case that it was difficult to foresee impartial justice. When the Associates failed to answer the court action, eviction notices were served in the summer of 1745.

The Horseneck Incident

Early in September of that year, agents of the proprietors discovered Samuel Baldwin at work in the Horseneck, "making great havoc with his sawmill of the best timber thereon." Baldwin declared that his rights stemmed from the old Indian deed. Baldwin's neighbors offered to pay his bail when he was arrested, but the woodchopper refused, saying that expensive lawsuits would ruin the settlers. Baldwin was sitting in the Essex County jail in Newark on Sunday, September 9, when rioting shook the town.

On that memorable Sunday afternoon, a band of about 150 men flooded into town armed with clubs, axes, and crowbars. When the sheriff tried to stop them, they brushed him aside and broke open the jail door and freed Baldwin. The intruders warned the sheriff that if anyone was arrested in retaliation they would return "with double the number of men" and might even bring a hundred Indians to lay waste to Newark.

Four months later the sheriff of Essex County made a rapid dash into the Horseneck section to arrest Nehemiah Baldwin, Robert Young, and Thomas Sarjent. He lodged them in the Newark jail on the night of January 15, 1745, charged with being ringleaders in the September fracas. The militia was ordered out as a precaution. Only about fifteen men responded, in evidence that Newarkers had no wish to fight neighbors and cousins. The next morning, when the sheriff ordered the militia to bring the prisoners before a judge, he was astounded at their "frivolous pretences, as that they had no horses, and could not go." After pleading and threatening, the sheriff finally found six volunteers. They started off to the judge's home with Baldwin in their midst.

A howling mob surrounded the sheriff and his six militiamen, and they released Baldwin. Later in the day, twenty-six militiamen were ordered to escort Young and Sarjent before the judge. By this time more than three hundred men blocked the street when the prisoners and their guards left the jail. The sheriff asked the crowd "the meaning of their meeting together in such a manner." The mob demanded the two prisoners. A judge stepped forward and "read the King's proclamation against riots and acquainted the people against the bad consequences of such proceedings."

Citizens Against Militia

The sheriff ordered two captains of the Newark militia to circulate among the throng, beating drums to call all militiamen to duty. Not one man responded. The drumming ceased. Silence fell over the Newark streets. Suddenly the leader of the rioters, Amos Roberts (or Robards), yelled: "Those who are upon my list follow me!" Most of the three hundred men in the streets fell in behind his horse.

The mob advanced on the militia, vowing that "if they were fired upon they would kill every man." The thin ranks of the militia stood firm, with firelocks at the ready. The order to fire never sounded; these advancing people were neighbors, not an enemy. The mob met restraint with viciousness. They beat the soldiers with clubs and swarmed toward the beleaguered sheriff, who stood alone before the jail door, his sword drawn. They brushed him aside, broke down the jail door, and freed the prisoners.

The Assembly convened in February just after the spectacle in the Newark streets. Governor Morris addressed the legislators and called the riots "high treason." Such occurrences, he said, were "likely to end in rebellion and the throwing off His Majesty's authority if timely measures be not taken to check the intemperance of a too licentious multitude." An Assembly spokesman announced that a

A BILL

IN THE

Chancery of *New-Jersey*,

AT THE SUIT OF

John Earl of *Stair*, and others, Proprietors
of the Eaſtern-Diviſion of *New-Jerſey*;

AGAINST

Benjamin Bond, and ſome other Perſons of *Elizabeth-Town*, diſtinguiſhed by the Name of the *Clinker Lot Right* Men.

WITH

Three large MAPS;. done from COPPER-PLATES.

To which is added;

The PUBLICATIONS

OF

The Council of Proprietors of *Eaſt New-Jerſey*,

AND

Mr. NEVILL's Speeches to the General Aſſembly,

CONCERNING

The *RIOTS* committed in NEW-JERSEY,

AND

The Pretences of the Rioters, and their Seducers.

Theſe Papers will give a better Light into the Hiſtory and Conſtitution of NEW-JERSEY, than any Thing hitherto publiſhed, the Matters whereof have been chiefly collected from Records.

Publiſhed by SUBSCRIPTION:

Printed by *James Parker*, in *New-York*, 1747; and a few Copies are to be Sold by him, and *Benjamin Franklin*, in *Philadelphia*; Price bound, and Maps coloured *Three Pounds*; plain and ſtitcht only, *Fifty Shillings*, Proclamation Money.

Title of the *Bill in the Chancery of New Jersey*, a document that sought to bring large numbers of rioters to the courts after the riots of 1745 and 1746. Benjamin Franklin, the page notes, was one of two authorized salesmen of the document—today one of New Jersey's rarest colonial publications.

militia bill had been introduced "to discourage things of that nature," but the proprietors complained that the bill fell far short of being an adequate remedy. The proprietors had a bill introduced in the Council providing that if twelve or more persons were meeting and refused to be dispersed when ordered to by a local or provincial officer, they should be judged felons and be put to death without benefit of clergy.

The Essex County rioters grew ever bolder. They presented a petition to the Assembly stating that hundreds of people held their lands by Indian title and begged that the King be asked to decide the controversy. Samuel Nevill, a judge, exclaimed that the petition was "a bold attempt upon the prerogative of the crown by calling in question of his Majesty's right and title to the soil of New Jersey."

The Riots Spread

The rioting quickly spread elsewhere. During the summer of 1746, unrest stirred in the hills of Hunterdon County, where Alexander and

Morris owned large tracts of land. That fall a mob broke into the Somerset County jail. By the spring of 1747, rioters in Morris County began driving people with proprietary titles from their houses. One March evening, a Morris group called at the home of Joseph Dalrimple and ordered him and his family to leave immediately. He pleaded that his wife was about to have a child, winning a stay of two weeks. A month later, militia officers of Morris County assembled to frighten off a mob that threatened to turn out Justice Daniel Cooper.

A Middlesex County crowd of about 150 men, armed with clubs, stormed into Perth Amboy in July to release John Bainbridge, Jr., who had been arrested for participating in the outbreak in Somerset County. John Deare, the Middlesex sheriff, wrote that the rioters marched behind two fiddlers. Deare's statement concluded:

> When I began to read the writ by which I had taken Bainbridge I was knocked down and suffered a Grievous Wound in my head. They also struck the Mayor, broke one of the Constable's head, beat several of the others and then violently with a Sledge and Iron Barr & Hatchet broke open the Outward and Inward Doors of the Gaol, took out the prisoner and carried him off Huzzaing.

The names of about twenty rioters were read to the Middlesex County grand jury a few days later. Judge Nevill asked that the troublemakers be indicted for high treason. The jury declined, saying it "would hardly indict them for a riot." Fear swept the colony. It was said that the rioting showed "contempt for his Majesty's authority." Leading proprietors urged parliamentary intervention. Judge Robert Hunter Morris wrote to England asking for troops to enforce law and order in the colonies. The situation had gone far beyond simple protesting by a few people. This was widespread rebellion.

The Seeds of the Revolution

It is difficult to assess the importance of the riots of 1745 and 1746. Yet here were sown some of the seeds of revolution to be reaped by all the colonies thirty years later. Public opinion simply would not tolerate the power that the proprietors had derived from a grant given long ago by a British king. The Assembly refused to provide the police force that the proprietors demanded, and the Crown was indifferent to struggle over New Jersey real estate. It takes only a little imagination to speculate on what might have happened if there had been royal troops in Newark on the night of September 19, 1745, when people of the Horseneck surged against the Essex County jail. Or suppose that red-coated soldiers had faced the mob of three hundred men in Newark on January 16, 1745? Suppose there had been no feeling that the rioters were neighbors, but rather enemies of the King? It is easy to conceive that the same kind of massacre that took place at Boston twenty-five years later could have occurred on the streets of Newark. But the time was not ripe for widespread revolution.

Governor Lewis Morris died on May 21, 1746, during the rioting. It might have been fitting that he should die in the midst of turbulence, for he had come to fame at the turn of the century, during another time of upheaval. His radicalism of 1700 had turned to conservatism by 1746, and the seventy-five-year-old governor had little influence when he died. His endless quarrels with the Assembly were not conducive to good government. The Assembly even refused to pay him for his last two years in office, charging that he had performed no services of value. The sick, sad, disillusioned governor had received the same treatment that he had helped levy against Lord Cornbury decades before.

Jonathan Belcher

Two temporary governors filled in after Lewis Morris died, and disorders lingered when Governor Jonathan Belcher arrived in August, 1747, as a permanent appointment. Born in Massachusetts and educated at Harvard, Belcher had been governor of Massachusetts from

1729 to 1741. When he heard, in April, 1746, that Lewis Morris was seriously ill, he promptly wrote to England, to ask that he be named governor of New Jersey as quickly as the post became vacant. Morris died a month after the letter was dispatched, and shortly thereafter Belcher had his wish.

New Jersey needed a strong and intelligent man, one able to sooth the divergent elements within the colony. Belcher's term began with much goodwill. West New Jersey Quakers supported him in the belief that the sympathy he had shown Massachusetts Quakers would make him understand their problems. East New Jersey residents, for their part, believed that his New England upbringing would make him sympathetic to town rule and instinctively opposed to the proprietors' demands for rents.

The proprietors mistrusted Belcher. Many of them felt that even before he became governor, he had encouraged Newark rioters not to appear in court in August, 1746, to face a test case. However, soon after his arrival, Belcher pleased the proprietors by promising that he would restore order—if he had to lead a regiment himself against the rioting elements. Then he made them wonder again in October. After first warning a delegation of rioters he meant to uphold the King's authority, Belcher changed his tone to kindness, explaining that "soft words turn away wrath, but the ringing of the nose brings forth blood."

Rioting continued in full swing when the legislators assembled in the fall of 1748. Belcher asked the Assembly to enact legislation to curb the lawlessness, declaring, "These things are done in sort of open rebellion against the King." The Assembly was at a serious crossroad. If it passed a law making rioting a crime of treason—as the proprietors wanted—most voters would be antagonized. If it did nothing, this could be considered as encouraging violence—and eventually this would force the governor to seek military aid from England to quell the disturbance.

During the autumn of 1748, the militants stepped up the stealing of timber from proprietary lands. James Alexander, a leading proprietor, wrote:

> As the locusts in Hungary eat up every green thing before them, so have the rioters destroyed all timber on the lands on the east side of the Passaic River, between Newark and Elizabethtown, belonging to many private persons here and in England, and now they have, in great number, armed, got over Passaic River into the lands of the proprietory of Pennsylvania, who have about twenty thousand acres of well timbered lands there.

Amos Roberts

The land riots brought to prominence an amazing, if little known, colonial figure—Amos Roberts (or Robards) of Newark. His name appeared often in official records and in the New York press. Among revolutionists he was "reverenced as much as if he had been a king," after he defied the Newark sheriff and the militia in the streets of Newark in January, 1745, to free the men charged in the Horseneck timber stealing. Roberts became increasingly bold. He led more than 150 mounted men into Perth Amboy in July, 1747, to free a prisoner.

Roberts persistently vowed his complete loyalty to the province and to the King. He wrote to the *New York Gazette* on January 23, 1749, accusing the proprietors of causing the "great disorders" and expressing his sorrow that they accused him of treason. He offered a reward of ten pounds to any man who could prove him a traitor—but said that he would continue to lead "free men" who resisted ejection from their lands. To evidence his regard for royal leadership, Roberts wrote: "God Bless the King that sits upon the British throne."

Even as Roberts professed his loyalty, he set up an illegal "kingdom" that was divided into wards, appointed his own tax collectors, set up his own courts, and organized his own militia. His followers were pledged to defend one another. One Abraham Shotwell related that Roberts told him "what a brave thing it was to join together to defend the country." Roberts declared in 1748 that if his followers had been attacked when they broke open the Perth Amboy jail they would have returned "and leveled Amboy with the ground." This was as defiant as the talk that later preceded the American Revolution.

Funds for the French and Indian War

Belcher's English superiors threatened in July, 1749, to send over a new governor backed by English troops. There was talk in London that New Jersey and New York should be reunited for the common good. Finally, late in 1751, Belcher received "smart orders" directing him to appoint an impartial commission to study the causes of rebellion and ordering the Assembly to cooperate in helping to bring about "peace and tranquility." By then the rioting was subsiding—not because the differences were less acute but because the first rumblings of the approaching French and Indian War were being heard.

In 1746, New Jersey had authorized ten thousand pounds to help support a British expedition against Canada. The Assembly acted reluctantly, fearing that the funds might be used to arm troops that would be turned against the squatters. John Low of Essex County, an assemblyman who admitted that he was a rioter himself, said: "Aye, perhaps you think I am a fool. Don't you think I see what one of the designs was, of raising these forces? Why I will tell you. When this expedition is over, these very men will be used to quell the rioters!"

As tensions between France and England deepened, New Jersey stood on the threshold of a new era. It would be clouded increasingly with bitterness toward England—and it would end in independence.

CHAPTER SIX

Colonial Pathway

The New Jersey that Lewis Morris had helped set free from government by the East and West New Jersey proprietors was vastly different from the New Jersey that developed after his death in 1746. Its internal growth was not rapid, but as a colony set between New York and Philadelphia—and midway between colonies to the north and to the south—New Jersey inevitably became a colonial pathway. Through this peninsula surged many people headed north or south. They brought with them new ideas and new thoughts. By 1750 New Jersey's role as a provincial pathway was well defined.

Wheaton J. Lane, who wrote the classic study of New Jersey's early transportation, *From Indian Trail to Iron Horse*, declared:

> New Jersey enjoyed a greater amount of intercolonial travel than any other part of America. The result was a wider tolerance and a greater interest in affairs beyond the immediate locality. Travellers commented upon the good-natured liberality of the native Jerseyman. Gradually the Puritanism of the northern towns broke down and the general cultures of East and West New Jersey became more and more alike. In the colonial period as well as later, New Jersey was literally a melting pot in which fused a culture more typically American than that of New England or the South.

The celebrated Swedish botanist Peter Kalm, who toured New Jersey and the other colonies between 1748 and 1751, was not im-

Transportation was an important matter in colonial New Jersey because of the colony's location between New York and Philadelphia. The earliest stage wagons across the state were crude vehicles with heavy wheels, which sometimes took as much as five days to cross between Burlington and the ferry at either Elizabeth or Jersey City. In bad weather the trip might take twice as long.

pressed with the roads between Philadelphia and New York. He left this description:

> The roads are good or bad according to the difference of the ground. In a sandy soil the roads are dry and good; but in a clayey one they are bad. The people here are likewise very careless in mending them. If a rivulet be not very great, they do not make a bridge over it; and travellers may do as well as they can to get over. Therefore many people are in danger of being drowned in such places, where the water is risen by a heavy rain.

Travel on those uncertain roads slowly evolved from foot travel to horseback riding to stage wagons. Settlers in the upper reaches of Somerset County brought their farm goods to New Brunswick on horseback, with a rider leading one or two horses on whose backs were fastened bags of grain. Ironmakers of Morris County brought ore from mine to forge in bags slung over the backs of horses and carried iron bars to Newark the same way.

The First Stage Line

Sometime before 1730 the stage wagon was devised. This vehicle made its first appearance in New Jersey; the first newspaper notice of it was in 1729, but it surely rolled before that. The stage wagon was a wide, heavy vehicle with huge wheels. A canvas top served to protect both passengers and cargo in bad weather. It was crude and back-wearying, but when hitched behind four to six horses, the "Jersey wagon" made fair speed.

The main road naturally lay between Burlington and Perth Amboy, the twin capitals where the legistlature met alternately each year. Passengers journeying between the capitals, as well as those traveling between New York and Philadelphia, desperately yearned for both increased comfort and speed, as well as a regular schedule.

Finally, in March, 1733, a regular route was advertised in the Philadelphia *American Weekly Mercury*. This was the first notice in America of a regular service. From this notice have grown all the schedules, timetables, and other controls so familiar in modern travel. The 1733 advertisement read:

> This is to give Notice unto Gentlemen, Merchants, Tradesmen, Travellers, and others, that Solomon Smith and James Moon of Burlington; keepeth two Stage-Waggons, intending to go from Burlington to Amboy, and back from Amboy to Burlington again. Once every week or offt'er if that Business presents. They have also a very good Store-house, very Commodious for the storing of any sort of Merchants Goods free from any Charges, where good care will be taken of all sorts of Goods by Solomon Smith and James Moon.

The Smith-Moon line apparently did not have much success, nor did a line established in 1739 between Trenton and Perth Amboy. Rival stage lines were begun in 1740 to link Bordentown and Perth Amboy, but by 1750 the chief route was between Trenton and New Brunswick, much shorter and easier on travelers. Still, even with roads in the best condition, it took four or five days to travel between New York and Philadelphia. This gave great importance to places along the way where people on the move might rest and eat.

The Sign of the Tavern

Taverns and inns sprang up along every highway. These had been emerging since a 1668 law ordered every New Jersey town to provide a place of refreshment for relief and entertainment of strangers. A

Because of the length of time it took to travel across the state, it was important to have inns and taverns along the way for overnight travelers. New Jersey's best-known colonial inn undoubtedly is the Indian King tavern in Haddonfield. The eastern part was built in 1750, and for the twenty-five years preceding the Revolution this was an important place of social and political gatherings in West New Jersey.

1739 law warned that taverns were for "accommodating strangers, travelers and other persons . . . and not for the encouragement of gaming, tippling, drunkenness and other vices so much of late practiced at such places." The tavern became the most vital place in town—the place of sheriff sales (sheriffs would sell off the property and possessions of those in debt) and court trials, the post office, and the center of excitement. Visitors and townspeople mingled in a main assembly room in front of the fireplace. Sleeping rooms above the taproom accommodated guests, two or more to a bed—first come, first served. Latecomers slept on the public-room floor, after all others had retired or gone home.

The tavern was usually the biggest place in town, and its sign was the most colorful. Owners used their imaginations in naming their places: the Sign of the College in Princeton, the Sign of the Green Tree in Trenton, the American House in Haddonfield, the Death of the Fox in Woodbury, the Bull's Head in Bound Brook, the Sign of the Seven Stars in Repaupo; the Rose and Crown, the Wheat Sheaf, and The Unicorn in Elizabeth; the Half Way Home in Bergen, the Black Horse in Perth Amboy, the White Hart and the Sign of the Red Lion in New Brunswick, and The Rising Sun and the Eagle in Newark.

Stagecoach travelers and horseback riders were not the only ones to take advantage of the taverns. Nearly every place had a large yard where drovers might herd their pigs or cattle for the overnight stop. The animals came from deep inland pastures and were driven over the dusty or muddy roads to the city markets. Often the drovers smelled so much like their beasts that they were not permitted even to enter the taproom, much less sleep in the tavern beds.

Glass Manufacture and Ironworks

Out-of-New Jersey travelers were not the only ones on the roads, for New Jersey's population had quadrupled between 1700 and 1745. A census in the latter year showed 61,383 inhabitants, about evenly split between the eastern and western sections. These people lived

This nineteenth-century engraving of the Dickerson Mine in Morris County shows the oldest iron mine in the northern part of the state. It was opened around 1700 and for more than a century supplied most of the ore used by iron forges in Morris County.

mainly on farms, but by 1750 ironmaking and glass manufacture were solidly in place beside leather tanning, distilling, and timber cutting as emerging New Jersey industries. The mountains of the north rang with the sounds of iron forges, and the people of the flatlands to the south were awakening to the fact that good glass could be made from the abundant sands.

Word reached Newark in about 1700 of a "black stone" (iron ore) being picked off the Succasunna plains by the Indians. Enterprising ironmakers went westward to exploit the ore. They built a forge in Hanover and brought their ore overland on horseback from Succasunna. The ore was melted down in Hanover and fashioned into U-shaped pigs (bars) that fitted over the backs of horses and mules. These were

The Batsto iron furnaces, made from bog iron, are a reminder of the days when iron was a vital industry in southern New Jersey. The iron kettle is also a mark of the Pine Barren ironworks.

laboriously carried eastward over the Watchung Mountains to the port at Newark, from where the pigs were shipped to England.

The northern hills were perfect for ironmaking. In addition to much iron ore on or near the surface, there was ample natural power and ready fuel. Restless streams tumbling from the mountains provided power for the waterwheels of the forges and furnaces. Hardwood forests supplied the huge amounts of fuel needed to convert ore to iron; a single forge fire could consume a thousand acres of woodland a year.

Other ironworks began, most of them using ore from the original Dickerson Mine opened about 1713 near Succasunna. Several ironworkers moved a few miles west from Hanover to start a forge in "the Hollow" (now Morristown). John Jackson started a forge at Dover in 1722, and an ironworks opened at Rockaway in about 1730. Iron had become so vital to these hill people by 1750 that they rebelled quietly in that year when a British law forbade rolling or slitting mills in the colonies. The Morris County ironmasters totally ignored the decree. Their revolt was more a matter of the pocketbook than of conscience, for when the American Revolution began, many of the ironmakers were outright Tories or suspected of being sympathetic to England.

Philadelphia moneymen looked to New Jersey iron as a source of wealth. Two of them, William Turner and Joseph Allen, built a forge in what is now High Bridge in 1742. That same year, Jonathon Robeson erected a 38-foot-high furnace at Oxford, deep in the forests to the north. A fourth Philadelphian, Charles Read, focused attention on South Jersey's bog iron in 1751, when he began to assemble an iron empire in the pine woodlands along the Mullica River and Great Egg Harbor River watersheds. Within fifteen years Read had erected busy ironworks at Taunton, Aetna, Atsion, and Batsto. All of them used bog iron.

Peter Hasenclever

The greatest of all New Jersey iron ventures began in 1763, when Peter Hasenclever came to the New York–New Jersey borderline to put together a major iron complex at Ringwood. The German-born

Peter Hasenclever (from an old painting). Hasenclever ran ironworks in the Ramapo Mountains. He came to New Jersey in 1763 and within six years had spent more than £54,000. He built a small empire in northern New Jersey that included iron forges at Charlotteburg, Long Pond, and Ringwood. His high style of living earned him the nickname the "Baron."

Hasenclever secured forty thousand pounds sterling, supplied by English capitalists. Before he left England, he shipped several hundred skilled German ironworkers and their families to New Jersey. Hasenclever bought fifty thousand acres in the wilds of the Ramapo Mountains and began fashioning an enterprise of astonishing proportions. He built bridges, buildings, towns, roads, and furnaces at Charlotteburg, Long Pond, and Ringwood. He raised an 860-foot-long dam to form Tuxedo Lake, said to be the first attempt in America to conserve water in wet seasons for use in dry seasons.

Hasenclever's freewheeling splurge commanded attention both in America and in England. Those who lived in the sprawling iron kingdom that he had founded called him "Baron" in tribute to his high style of living. His English backers were appalled at his quick spending of £54,000—£14,000 more than they had granted him. They recalled Hasenclever in 1769, but by then he had put together an iron industry that lasted for over two centuries.

Casper Wistar

Another long-lived New Jersey industry began in 1739, when Casper Wistar of Philadelphia opened America's first successful glass factory in Salem County. Earlier glassmaking attempts—at Jamestown, Virginia, and Salem, Massachusetts, for example—had been short-lived failures. Wistar had no practical knowledge of glassmaking, but as a leading colonial maker of brass buttons he knew markets and recognized that his Philadelphian neighbors would buy American glassware if it was available. He knew as well that fine South Jersey sand could be melted into glass through use of the ample wood in the Pine Barrens.

Wistar made up for his lack of skill by importing four journeymen glassmakers from Rotterdam. His contract with them limited them to teaching glassmaking to him and his son Richard, "and no one else." The Rotterdam experts demanded, and received, one third of all profits. Everyone prospered. Wistarware became much sought after in all the counties. The town of Wistarburg that sprang up around the

114

glass factory became known as the "cradle of American glassmaking." Workers moved elsewhere in South Jersey, journeyed on to New England, and eventually moved westward over the Allegheny Mountains to establish their own glassworks in Ohio and elsewhere.

More People, New Counties

New Jersey's political pattern was altered by growth. As more and more people arrived, especially in the northwestern mountains, complaints grew of the distances to the county seats. An area that broke away from Burlington County in 1714 was named Hunterdon County in honor of the popular Governor Robert Hunter. This new county extended from Trenton north to the New York border, including most of modern Mercer, Morris, Sussex, and Warren counties. Eventually people in the north lands objected to traveling to Hunterdon's county courts in Flemington, and in 1739 Morris County was set off and named for Governor Lewis Morris. The residents also recognized the governor by calling their county seat Morristown.

Two other counties were formed before the Revolution. In 1748, a large piece was broken away from Salem County to form Cumberland County, with the county seat at Bridgeton. Five years later those who lived in the north of Morris County grew so completely disenchanted with the long trip to Morristown for court sessions that they split away an area comprising all of modern Sussex and Warren counties. They called this new county Sussex and set the county seat at Log Gaol (now Johnsonburg). The creation of Hunterdon, Morris, Cumberland, and Salem counties brought the total of counties to thirteen. No others would be created until 1824. (New Jersey now has twenty-one counties.)

The Churches

None of the changes in New Jersey was more compelling than the transformations in religion. For one thing, the Puritans of East New Jersey gradually became Presbyterians, a change that had been in the

It is interesting to note that the first presidents of two of the Ivy League's "Big Three" (Princeton, Yale, and Harvard) were Newark men. Abraham (Abrahamus) Pierson was the son of Newark's first spiritual leader. He became head of what is now Yale University, known in its founding days as the College of Connecticut.

making since 1668 when the Reverend Abraham Pierson, Jr., came to Newark as co-pastor with his father, whom he succeeded in 1678. In 1701, Mr. Pierson became the first President of the Collegiate School of Connecticut (now Yale University). By 1700 the separation of church and civil affairs was well under way in Newark and elsewhere. That year Newark chose its new minister through a joint committee of three townspeople and three church people rather than by a town committee. The new minister's salary came solely from church members rather than from the town at large, as in the past.

Newark became the center of New Jersey Presbyterianism in 1737, when a young minister named Aaron Burr was named pastor of Newark's First Church. He seemed little more than a boy, but Burr was a Yale graduate, and shortly before Christmas, 1736, he had been asked to preach on trial basis in Newark. He was so brilliant that he was installed as permanent minister on January 25, 1737, just twenty-one days after his twenty-first birthday.

The Church of England (the Anglican Church) grew ever stronger after the founding, in 1702, of St. Mary's Church in Burlington, the center of West New Jersey Quakerism. At about the same time a small Anglican congregation began meeting in Elizabethtown, with the Reverend John Brooke as vicar. The Elizabethtown Anglicans at first shared a meetinghouse, but soon they began building their own St. John's Church. Constructed of bricks, it was not finished for ten years. Governor Cornbury applied constant pressure on the Anglicans and put both Mr. Brooke and another Anglican, the Reverend Thoroughgood Moore of Burlington, in jail in New York. They es-

Christ Church, Shrewsbury, New Jersey, is a fine example of colonial architecture. The parish was organized in 1702 and the first church erected about 1705. The present building, dating from 1769, was used as a barracks by Continental troops during the Revolutionary War. It was consecrated in 1845. Many colonial treasures are contained in it.

This 1870 engraving shows Colonel Josiah Ward taking in his wheat on a Sunday in 1733, before rains ruined the crop. Presbyterians on the way to church were appalled.

caped and fled for England. But New Jersey's first two Anglican vicars both perished when their ship was lost at sea.

Mr. Brooke's death brought to Elizabethtown the Reverend Edward Vaughn, destined to be rector of St. John's for thirty-eight years. Mr. Vaughn was a man to be reckoned with in that staunchly Puritan town. He was well liked, and his ministry steadily drew converts away from the Presbyterian Church. It was said that some who joined St. John's were attracted by the fact that Mr. Vaughn's marriage to a wealthy widow enabled him to pay most church expenses himself.

As one church grew, others suffered losses. The founding of Newark's Episcopal congregation was a case in point. It came about because Colonel Josiah Ogden was irked by Presbyterian rigidity that interfered with his own needs. He was a leading churchman, descended from the founders of Newark, but he was as practical as he was pious. Late in the summer of 1733, continuous rains threatened his wheat, which was already cut. When the hot sun broke through on a Sunday morning and dried the grain, the colonel led his family into the field and harvested the wheat in defiance of church laws against working on Sunday. Presbyterians on the way to the meetinghouse were horrified.

Church fathers rebuked Ogden sternly for violating Sunday laws. The harsh trial and the severity of the public scolding caused Ogden to leave the church and split Newark asunder. Many others dropped out of the Presbyterian ranks in sympathy, and soon the dissenters founded an Episcopal church, chartered as Trinity Church in 1746. The new church, contained so many descendants of founding families that an agreement was reached whereby part of the original town military ground was set aside for their use. Trinity Church received a half acre on the northern end of the training ground and there the congregation built a handsome stone church, topped by a ninety-five-foot white steeple that dominated the village green and gave Newark a "New England" look. Trinity Church still stands on that green in the midst of downtown Newark's skyscrapers.

The Great Awakening

Religious zeal struck all of the colonies in the middle years of the eighteenth century. Evangelists roaming the colonies from Georgia to Massachusetts passed through New Jersey constantly in the 1740's, stirring what was known as the "Great Awakening." Religious revivalism was mixed with outspoken defiance of established church order. No church escaped the effects.

No individual attained greater stature during the Great Awakening than the Reverend Theodore J. Frelinghuysen of New Jersey's Raritan Valley. When he came from Germany in 1720 to serve four congregations in the valley (between present-day Somerville and New Brunswick), Mr. Frelinghuysen found most of his Dutch church members unwilling to accept new ideas. They did not like his emotion-stirring sermons; he persisted in the face of strong warnings that his sermons were not "traditional."

William Warren Sweet, a major religious authority in the United States, declared in his *Religion in Colonial America* that Frelinghuysen was "the first outstanding revivalist" in the Middle Colonies. He wrote: "The well-to-do, the kind who generally hold the principal offices in churches, were scandalized; the poorer people and the younger generation were inclined to support their young and enthusiastic Domine." Frelinghuysen's impassioned sermons profoundly changed every Dutch Reformed Church in the colonies. His call for an understandable faith attracted large numbers of new people to his church.

Presbyterian fervor was stirred in the early 1740's by the Reverend George Whitefield, the most powerful evangelist of his time and one of the greatest in all history. He preached often in New Jersey, moving rapidly from town to town, from Greenwich to Newark and from Salem to New Brunswick. Whitefield attracted tremendous crowds. A newspaper account of May 1, 1740, told of seven thousand people gathered to hear him in New Brunswick (at a time when there were only sixty thousand people in New Jersey). Whitefield wrote often in his diary of his stops in New Jersey. He recorded, in November, 1740, a meeting in Newark where "the word fell like a hammer and like fire! What a weeping was there! One poor creature in particular was ready to sink into the earth!" He wrote of his stop in New Brunswick: "God's power was so much amongst us in the afternoon sermon that had I proceeded, the cries and groans of the congregation I believe would have drowned out my voice."

The College of New Jersey

The evangelical stirrings had lasting effects, for they led directly to the founding of two major colleges—the College of New Jersey (now Princeton University) and Queens College (now Rutgers, the State University). Only nine colleges were founded in America before the American Revolution. New Jersey was the only colony to have two.

120

The Reverend Aaron Burr of Newark became president of the College of New Jersey in 1747, after the death of the college's founder, who had served only four months. Mr. Burr put the college on sound footing. (*Below*) Nassau Hall, built between 1753 and 1756, "the largest stone building in all the colonies." This picture shows Nassau Hall within a decade of its construction. To the right is the President's House, where Mr. Burr lived. This house also still stands on the Princeton University campus.

Aaron Burr, Jr., was graduated from the College of New Jersey in 1772. He later became Vice President of the United States.

The College of New Jersey was founded by Presbyterians of the middle colonies who believed that their young ministers ought to be trained nearby instead of in New England or European colleges. Its first site was the town of Elizabeth—as Elizabethtown was officially called since 1740. The college was chartered on October 22, 1746, to hold classes in the parlor of the Reverend Jonathan Dickinson, pastor of the Presbyterian church in Elizabeth. Mr. Dickinson died within four months, and the Reverend Aaron Burr invited the eight college students to Newark to finish the year. Classes met in the courtroom above the county jail on Broad Street.

The college continued in Newark. At the first commencement, on November 9, 1748, an honorary degree was given Governor Jonathan Belcher, a staunch friend of the struggling institution. Of the first six graduates, five became ministers. The sixth was Richard Stockton, who chose to study law. Stockton became one of New Jersey's five signers of the Declaration of Independence in 1776.

Mr. Burr recognized that the College of New Jersey could not prosper in Newark. He hoped that New Brunswick would offer a place for the college, but when he asked for a bond of a thousand pounds, ten acres of cleared ground, and two hundred acres of woodland, New Brunswick would not meet the requirements. Princeton accepted the conditions in 1753. There the College of New Jersey raised its new home, acclaimed as "the largest stone building in all the colonies." It was named Nassau Hall and the college moved there from Newark in November of 1756. Mr. Burr died soon after. His name lives on chiefly through his son, Aaron Burr, Jr., who was born in Newark. The Vice President of the United States under Thomas Jefferson, Aaron Burr's political life became clouded when he killed Alexander Hamilton in a duel at Weehawken in 1804.

Queens College

New Brunswick, proud of its growth, was disappointed that the College of New Jersey could not be brought to the banks of the Raritan River. James Alexander had written in 1730 that land was worth "near as great a price as so much ground in the heart of New York." There was pleasure in 1766 when a state charter was granted for the start of Queen's College under the auspices of the Dutch Reformed Church. The trustees acquired a former tavern, the Sign of the Red Lion, as their college building and named Frederick Frelinghuysen as their lone faculty member. He was enough: the first graduating class in 1774 had only one graduate.

The colleges in Princeton and New Brunswick really were seminaries, dedicated to training ministers. They were not intended for the average person. For that matter, there were no public schools at the time. Some rudimentary education was given to very young children by ministers. But boys usually left school at age seven or eight to work on the family farm, and education for girls was considered a frill. Except for the wealthy, who sent their sons to private academies, colonial America verged on illiteracy.

123

Slavery in New Jersey

Education, even in the severely limited form of the eighteenth century, offered no hope for New Jersey's forgotten people—the Negro slaves and the supposedly free Indians. Slavery had existed from the time when the first Dutch plantations rose along the Hudson and Delaware rivers. The Puritans who came from Long Island or New England had few slaves, more a matter of practicality than religious conviction; most of these immigrants were poor themselves and had neither the time nor the money to bother with slaves. The Quakers of western New Jersey at first kept a few slaves, although there was a feeling that the system was wrong. In 1737, when New Jersey's population was 47,402 people, there were 3,981 slaves—about 8 percent of the population. New Jersey's colonial laws made no distinction between black and Indian slaves.

Queen Anne sought to make slavery a permanent fixture. In her instructions to Lord Cornbury in 1702 she directed him to encourage the Royal African Company of England to provide "a constant and sufficient supply of merchantable Negroes, at moderate rates." He was ordered to "take special care" to secure prompt payment for the slaves and to seek a monopoly in New Jersey for a royal slave dealer. The Queen asked for an annual report on the number of Negroes imported and the prices that they brought.

The black slave lived a harsh and degrading life. Legislation constantly sought to curb his free movement and to ensure crushing punishment. If, for example, a slave were to buy alcoholic drinks or other wares, the seller, if white, was merely fined. The slave who bought was whipped severely. Since imprisonment meant economic loss for an owner, savage whippings were used to keep slaves in line. Special courts were provided for slave trials, and not until after the Revolution did New Jersey decree that major criminal offenses be punishable equally for both whites and blacks.

One recorded incident of a Negro who was convicted of murder in Monmouth County in 1694 underscores the incredible brutality visited upon a black criminal. The presiding justice addressed the slave thusly:

> Caesar, thou art found guilty by thy county of those horrid crimes that are laid to thy charge; therefore, the court doth judge that thou, the said Caesar, shall return to the place from whence thou comest, and from thence to the place of execution, when thy right hand shall be cut off and burned before thine eyes. Then thou shalt be hanged up by the neck till thou are dead, dead, dead; then thy body shall be cut down to ashes in a fire, and so the Lord have mercy on thou soul, Caesar.

White owners assured one another that they treated their slaves well, at least in comparison with slaves on southern plantations. A memoir by a Dutch farmer of Bergen County declared nostalgically that slaves were "generally treated as members of the family; living under the same roof and even sitting down at the same table." Slaves and masters often worked side by side as a matter of economic necessity. Slaves also worshiped in the same churches as their masters, but they wore cast-off clothing and occupied seats in the gallery or in the rear of the church. There were no black churches until the nineteenth century. When a slave died he was buried in a corner of the church graveyard, "lest when the trumpet of Resurrection sounded there should be a disagreeable confusion of persons."

That slaves were not as happy as their white masters liked to believe is evident in the fact that many ran away. There is no way of measuring the exact numbers, but so many blacks fled that the legislature often discussed proper rewards for those who returned runaway slaves. Newspapers in New York and Philadelphia always carried advertisements for escaped blacks. William Nelson, editor of the *Archives of the State of New Jersey*, published by the New Jersey Historical Society, commented on these advertisements:

> The curious garbs worn by the runaways—relics of finery indicating often their former gentle position, or the sterner stuff

wherewith the common people were clad; the references to branding, showing the prevalence of that barbarous custom as a punishment for crime; the peculiar descriptions of some of the servants—the "Leering down Look," "proud hambling Gate," "walks Crimpling," "he is so prodigious a Lyar that if observed he may easily be discovered by it," "with a long Nose and a wild Look," "goes crooked and groans very much in his sleep," "speaks by clusters," "talks West Country," etc.—all throw a flood of light on the conditions of the toiling masses.

Negro labor was especially common on Bergen County's Dutch farms, although slaves were found in most of New Jersey. It was written in 1758 that nearly every house in Perth Amboy "swarmed with black slaves." When Samuel Finley, president of the College of New Jersey, died in 1766, his estate included "two negro women, a negro man and three negro children." All of them were offered for sale, as just so much property.

A few voices stirred against the evils of slavery, and no voice in the American colonies was stronger in opposition to slavery than that of the Reverend John Woolman of Mount Holly. Born in 1720 into a Quaker family, Woolman decided early in life that slavery was wrong. When he was twenty-three years old, Woolman was ordered by an employer to sign a bill of sale for a slave. The young Quaker refused, saying, "I believe slave keeping to be a practice inconsistent to the Christian religion."

Woolman traveled extensively throughout the colonies, preaching against slavery, in the Deep South as well as in New England. In 1754 his treatise, "Some Considerations in the Keeping of Negroes," spoke bitterly of slavery as being completely contrary to Scripture. Woolman insisted that "liberty was the natural right of all men equally," and in 1759 he journeyed among Quaker congregations to urge them "to labor against buying and keeping slaves." The Society of Friends, chiefly because of Woolman, barred slave owners from membership

Watercolor of Broad Street, Newark, in 1745, the earliest known view of the town. Trinity Church is on the right, and only a few cottages can be seen beside the muddy ruts of Newark's chief street.

before the Revolution. Woolman died in 1773 in England of smallpox. A year later the New Jersey Assembly seriously considered bills to prohibit the importation of slaves. The bills were not adopted. Although thoughts of independence were sweeping the land, there were few who believed that *all* men were created equal.

CHAPTER SEVEN

Colony in the Middle

Governor Jonathan Belcher's rule in New Jersey ended with his death on August 31, 1757, a year after suffering a paralytic stroke at the 1756 commencement of the College of New Jersey. He had recovered somewhat through use of an electrical apparatus sent him by Benjamin Franklin, but his life was shortened by worries brought on by the growing French and Indian War.

New Jersey's assemblymen had behaved in their traditional pattern, balking continuously at helping the British war effort in the French and Indian War. They pleaded that the province was too poor to supply funds, especially with the English ban on new paper money. Their obstinacy was strengthened by the fact that the soldiers of Pennsylvania and New York guarded the frontiers against Indian attacks, and thus they felt safe. New Jersey legislators used the same leverage on the Crown that they had long used on their governors: Unless they got their way in money matters, there would be no help.

Five hundred New Jersey militiamen were sent to upper New York in 1755 under the command of a native son, Colonel Peter Schuyler. Then, in July, 1755, the war struck close to home when French and Indian troops slaughtered General Edward Braddock's army in western Pennsylvania. Bands of Indians struck deep into Sussex County during the fall of 1755 and the spring of 1756. Belcher dispatched the provincial militia to Sussex, and the frightened legislature voted funds to build stone blockhouses along the upper Delaware River. Yet even fear did not loosen the purse strings. In 1757 New Jersey was

New Jersey's chief figure in the French and Indian War was Peter Schuyler, who lived on a large estate near Newark. He actively led New Jersey troops in the Northern campaigns.

the only colony that had refused to contribute its quota of men or money to the King's cause, arguing that restrictions on issuing new paper money would cause too much financial burden.

Barracks for the British

However, the Assembly acted quickly when the English government threatened to house six hundred soldiers in private homes in Newark, Perth Amboy, and Elizabeth. Funds were approved to build barracks in Elizabeth, New Brunswick, Perth Amboy, Burlington, and Trenton at a cost of fourteen hundred pounds sterling each. The first troops moved into the Trenton barracks late in 1758, and the five were completed and occupied by 1759. All but the Trenton barracks have disappeared. That served later for English and Hessian troops during the Revolution. Now fully restored, the old barracks is an attraction for thousands of visitors each year, including hundreds of school classes.

129

The "Old Barracks" in Trenton (an Earl Horter engraving). The Old Barracks housed British troops during the French and Indian War and during the Revolution, when Hessians were quartered during the Battle of Trenton. Today the Old Barracks is a favorite visiting place for the schoolchildren of New Jersey.

America's First Indian Reservation

Troubles with the Indians reached a peak in the spring of 1758, when Governor Francis Bernard arrived in New Jersey from England. He promptly opened negotiations with the Indians, reaching a peace treaty at Easton, Pennsylvania, in August of 1758. Three months later Governor Bernard helped establish America's first Indian reservation at Brotherton (now Indian Mills) in Burlington County. The dwindling remnant of the Lenni-Lenape tribe—not more than two hundred—gathered together at Brotherton in the fall of 1758 and the winter of 1759. The Indians enthusiastically tilled the fields and fished the streams for a time, but their affairs steadily worsened. Reports of poor "naked children" and "starving squaws" reached surrounding towns. Finally, in 1802, the Indians sold the land back to New Jersey, paid their debts, and left New Jersey forever, to join other Indians at Lake Oneida in New York.

Messages of gratitude poured into the governor's office after the peace of 1758, but within a year Bernard wrote that unless his salary was boosted he would seek to be transferred elsewhere. He asked that his salary be paid directly by the Crown rather than forcing him each year to stand before the Assembly, literally begging for his salary. Bernard's struggles to support his growing family forced him to accept the governorship of Massachusetts early in 1760.

A new day had come for England and its colonies. King George III had brought to the throne a belief that England must govern its colonies sternly. The French and Indian War had drained the treasury and doubled England's national debt. King George and his advisers insisted that the colonies must pay taxes to help support their government.

Mural in the Library at Trenton State College depicts Governor Francis Bernard with representatives of the Lenni-Lenape Indians at Easton, Pennsylvania, in 1758.

Ben Franklin's Son Becomes Governor

William Franklin inherited that English philosophy when he was appointed governor of New Jersey in 1763. The thirty-three-year-old governor was Benjamin Franklin's son and was respected in his own right for his intelligence and diplomatic skills. He was sympathetic to both American and British concerns and might well have served as a bridge between the countries. Instead it fell to his lot to sit in on the complete break between England and the colonies.

The New Jersey of 1763 was unknown to Franklin. For that matter, it was not well known by those who lived within its borders. When Samuel Smith of Burlington wrote New Jersey's first history in 1765, he paid particular attention to the fact that New Jersey was overwhelmed by strong neighbors:

> As the province has very little foreign trade on bottoms of its own, the produce of all kinds for sale, goes chiefly to New York and Philadelphia; much of it is there purchased for markets abroad, but some consumed among themselves. The inhabitants as to dress and manners, form themselves much after the neighbouring provinces; the western, about as far as the tide flows up the Delaware, those of Pennsylvania; the remainder those of New York.

Smith estimated that there were about a hundred thousand people in New Jersey in 1765, living in sixty towns and villages with definite place names or in another thirty-five crossroad hamlets known only by the name of the tavern on the corner or the most prominent citizen in the scattered houses along the way. By 1765, people were everywhere in the province—even beyond the Kittatinny Mountains to the northwest and along the barren seacoast. Farmers found riches in the soil of Salem, Gloucester, and Cumberland counties. Hunterdon County supplied flour for both New York and Philadelphia. The Raritan Valley's residents grew wheat in large quantities for New York. Essex County raised much farm produce, although Smith noted that "their plantations are too high in value to be generally large."

Smith noted that the seacoast was still little settled because of "a great extent of salt meadows, swamps and marshes and being exposed to the northeast winds." He added:

> Almost the whole extent of the province adjoining on the Atlantick, is barrens, or nearly approaching it; yet there are scattering settlements all along the coast, the people subsisting in great part by raising cattle in the bog, undrained meadows and marshes, and selling them to graziers, and cutting down the cedars; there were originally plenty of both the red and white sorts . . . They are now much worked out. Another means of subsistence along the coast, is the plenty of fish and oysters, these are carried to New York and Philadelphia markets. It is thought, no considerable whale-fishery might be formed there; on the banks [Cape May] the New England men frequently fish with success. The barrens or poor land, generally continues from the sea up into the province, thirty miles or more, and this nearly the whole extent from east to west; so that there are many thousand acres, that will never serve much of the purposes of agriculture; consequently when the pines and cedars are generally gone (they are so already in many places) this will not be of much value.

Governor William Franklin reached New Jersey on February 25, 1763. He first met the public in Perth Amboy, hailed by "a numerous concourse of people." He spoke very briefly: "I thank you for your kind congratulations. The esteem which you so gratefully and justly express for my predecessor is no less agreeable to me. And wherever I may reside, which is as yet uncertain, I shall be glad for every opportunity of showing my regard for the city of Perth Amboy."

England applied pressures for funds. The Sugar Act of 1764 enforced duties on molasses and other items and prohibited all trade between American colonies and the French West Indies. A severe economic depression hit the middle and northern colonies, and on the horizon was something far worse: the Stamp Act.

The Stamp Act

Parliament announced that effective November 1, 1765, colonists must place tax stamps on all legal documents, printed matter, licenses, playing cards, and even university degrees. The Stamp Act also stipulated that receipts from stamp sales would pay governmental and military expenses—including the governor's salary. Jerseymen who had kept governors in line for years by threatening their incomes were doubly appalled.

New Jersey seethed with anger. Even a conservative such as Cortland Skinner of Perth Amboy (who during the Revolution became an active Tory) could write: "Everything here is in the greatest confusion, and the first of November is dreaded." Governor Franklin named William Coxe of Burlington as the stamp officer. When Coxe sought to rent a stamp office, he was refused. He was asked, "Who would ensure that the house would not be pulled down?" Coxe's friends begged him to resign, even though he would forfeit a three-thousand-pound bond he had put up.

Angry opposition flared. On September 21, 1765, a newspaper was published at the printing office of James Parker in Woodbridge. New Jersey had no previous newspaper and this one, the *Constitutional Courant*, started and ended on the same day. Its heading declared that the paper contained "matters interesting to liberty—but no wise repugnant to loyalty." A commentator of the time said the *Courant* was "the most remarkable of inflammatory papers" aimed at the Stamp Act. Agents of the King suppressed the paper immediately.

New Jersey's lawyers met at Perth Amboy in September to seek ways of avoiding the Stamp Act. They unanimously resolved not to buy any stamps or to do any business that required stamps, declaring that their "private interest" should be second to the public good. They

The dining room in Morven is furnished in early-eighteenth century style. It is a favorite place for visitors interested in the colonial period.

Morven, built sometime before 1760 by the Stockton family, is a good example of Georgian elegance. It was owned by the Stocktons for more than two centuries and since the 1950's has been the home of the governor of New Jersey.

also declared themselves opposed to "all indecent and riotous behavior." Interestingly, Virginia's George Washington also thought that not using the stamps was the best way of getting the Act repealed.

Other colonies were not interested in peaceful opposition. Massachusetts, the most radical, invited all colonies to send delegates to a Stamp Act Congress in New York on October 7 for a unified display of colonial protest. Robert Ogden, speaker of the New Jersey Assembly, hesitated in the belief that a colonial protest ought not to come so quickly. Richard Stockton of Princeton, a young lawyer, said that if New Jersey failed to attend "we shall not only look like a speckled bird among our sister colonies, but shall say implicitly that we think it no oppression." It was agreed to send three delegates—Ogden, Hendrick Fisher of Somerset County, and Joseph Borden of Burlington County. Ogden was one of two delegates (the other being from radical Massachusetts) who voted against a "Declaration of the Rights and Grievances of the Colonists" adopted by the congress. Ogden opposed a united petition to King George, preferring protests from individual colonies. He returned to New Jersey to face such wrath that he was forced to resign from his Assembly seat.

When there were no stamps in New Jersey by November 1, William Coxe said that bringing in the stamps "would occasion disorder and bloodshed." Equally, declared the candid Coxe, "I should be injured both in person and estate." Franklin called the Assembly to meet in Burlington, believing that no violence would occur in Quaker West Jersey.

The Assembly passed eleven resolutions condemning the Stamp Act, modeling their protest along the lines of the Stamp Act Congress declarations. The Assembly repeated the long-held belief that the *Concessions and Agreements* of 1664 and 1676 provided for taxation by the General Assembly only. The assemblymen reminded King George that his subjects were "entitled to all the inherent rights and liberties of his natural born subjects" in England, including the right "that no taxes be imposed on them but with their own consent personally, or by their representatives."

Business Without Stamps

The Sons of Liberty appeared in New Jersey for the first time in December. Two members from Woodbridge threatened Coxe, saying that if he did not resign they would treat him "in such a way and manner as perhaps will be disagreeable both to yourself and to us." Coxe resigned and joined the Sons of Liberty in a toast to the King and "confusion to every American Stamp Master unless he resigns his abhorred and detestable office." Coxe's resignation attested to the fact that his safety was on the line.

Disorder increased as the winter wore on. In February the Woodbridge Sons of Liberty said they would oppose the Stamp Act with their lives and fortunes. Elizabeth "Sons" erected a gallows and reserved its rope for the first stamp distributor. Piscataway Sons of Liberty said they agreed to peace if it could be accomplished "without suffering any imposition on our just rights and liberty." Opponents gathered in Hunterdon and Monmouth counties, and in Sussex County one thousand people loudly expressed their hatred for the stamps. Lawyers became firmer in February, 1766, declaring that if the Act was not repealed by April 1, they would resume business without stamps. Some lawyers in Elizabeth and in Cumberland and Sussex counties resumed work immediately, without stamps.

England's House of Commons repealed the Stamp Act on February 21, 1766. The news reached New Jersey on April 3, 1766, and six weeks later "an elegant entertainment" was held in Burlington. Governor Franklin and the inhabitants toasted English royalty and the Parliament in a festivity "conducted with the greatest order and decorum." The Sons of Liberty in Woodbridge combined celebration of the repeal with King George's birthday early in June, "and the most firm loyalty seemed to glow in every breast."

The Townshend Act

The triumph was short-lived. In May, 1767, England's Chancellor of the Exchequer, Charles Townshend, announced that new duties would be imposed on glass, paper, red and white lead, and tea, with duties to be collected in colonial ports. Proceeds would be used to help maintain governors and judges in America. Colonists everywhere joined in nonimportation agreements to protest the so-called Townshend Acts. New Jersey's Assembly wrote King George directly, unknown to Governor Franklin, that settlers in America carried the "rights and liberties" of all Englishmen—especially the right of taxation only "by themselves or their representatives." Franklin was severely reprimanded by his English superiors for such bold action by his subjects. He answered that "no force on earth is sufficient to make the assemblies acknowledge by any act of theirs that the Parliament has a right to impose taxes on America."

The Townshend Acts were repealed on March 5, 1770, ironically on the same day that five persons were killed on the Boston Common by British soldiers in the Boston Massacre. As a symbol of England's right to tax colonists, the relatively light tax on tea remained. Tea became something socially unacceptable, and later it would boil into a series of protesting "tea parties."

New Jersey assemblymen rebelled at supporting British soldiers in the colony's five barracks. When Governor Franklin was able to rid the colony of troops in the fall of 1772, the Assembly grudgingly voted to pay his salary. Franklin scolded them for "a fatal sentiment that has long and unhappily prevailed in this province, that every measure which must be attended with expense and has not a tendency to benefit every part of the province equally, ought not to be adopted by the legislature." He said this placed the province "shamefully behind all others in its trade, roads, bridges, public buildings, and such other improvement that note a sensible and spirited people."

The governor grew increasingly unhappy. A rising resentment against his father Benjamin in England made it difficult for William ever to win a promotion. In 1772, William wrote his father that he would like to be appointed the governor of Barbados, but realized that he had no chance while his English superiors were "so much displeased with your conduct." In January, 1774, England removed Benjamin Franklin as head of the post office in America. Benjamin warned the governor that he would be better off "well settled on your farm" in Burlington.

William Franklin sided against rebellious Americans when "Indians" boarded the ship *Dartmouth* in Boston harbor in December of 1773 and dumped its cargo of tea in the famous Boston Tea Party. When the British closed the port of Boston in June, 1774, and placed it under martial law, William defended the action in a letter to Benjamin. Within a year they no longer spoke to one another.

The Continental Congress

The people of New Jersey gradually took matters into their own hands. On June 6, 1774, a town meeting in Monmouth County resolved that "the cause of Boston was the cause of all." On June 11, a meeting in

The mural in the Essex County courthouse shows the foreman of the Grand Jury rebuking Chief Justice Smythe and other members of the court for declaring, in November, 1774, that the colonists were protesting against "imaginary tyranny, 3,000 miles distant."

Essex County reaffirmed the Monmouth support of Boston and called for a Continental Congress to petition the King. Quickly, other groups met in Bergen, Morris, Hunterdon, Middlesex, Sussex, and Monmouth. Representatives were summoned to meet on July 21 at New Brunswick. Anguished at this turn of events, Franklin wrote Lord Dartmouth that there was "no forseeing the consequences."

Seventy-two delegates gathered in New Brunswick. First swearing allegiance to the King and shunning independence, they then called Parliament's taxation laws "unconstitutional and oppressive." They agreed to join other colonies in a Continental Congress. Chosen to represent New Jersey were James Kinsey, John DeHart, Stephen Crane, William Livingston, and Richard Smith. Three of them—Livingston, DeHart, and Crane—came from Essex County, where a rebellious spirit long had flourished.

A mood of independence filled the air. In November, 1774, Chief Justice Frederick Smyth told a Newark grand jury that protesting

Drawing from Ellis and Snyder's *Brief History of New Jersey* depicts Greenwich tea party in 1774.

colonists were "guarding against imaginary tyranny, 3,000 miles distant." He warned the jury that it ought to study "real tyranny at our own doors." Grand jurors who once might have sat in awe of a King's judge informed Smyth in words preserved in the New York *Journal:*

> We cannot think, sir, the taxes imposed upon us by our fellow subjects, in a legislature in which we are not represented, is imaginary, but that it is real and actual tyranny. We cannot think, sir, that depriving us of the inestimable right of trial by jury—seizing our persons, and carrying us for trial to Great Britain, is a tyranny merely imaginary. Nor can we think with your honor that destroying charters, and changing our forms of government is a tyranny altogether ideal.
>
> In a word, sir, we cannot persuade ourselves that the fleet now blocking up the Port of Boston, consisting of ships built of real English oak and solid iron, and armed with cannon and ponderous metal, with actual powder and ball, nor the army lodging in the town of Boston, and the fortification thrown about it (substantial and formidable realities) are all creatures of the imaginations. These, sir, are but a few of the numerous grievances under which America now groans.

New Jersey's Own Tea Party

A month later violence exploded in the little town of Greenwich off Delaware Bay. On December 12, 1774, the master of the English brig *Greyhound* sailed into Greenwich after deciding not to risk his cargo of tea in Philadelphia. He unloaded and stored the tea in Dan Bowen's cellar. On the night of December 22, more than twenty "Indians" (Cumberland County men disguised as Indians) took the tea from Dan Bowen's cellar and burned it in the streets.

Seven alleged Greenwich arsonists were placed on trial in April, 1775. None needed to be overly concerned about the outcome. The sheriff, Johnathan Elmer, was the brother of one defendant. The jury was headed by Daniel Elmer, a nephew of both the sheriff and a defendant. A verdict of innocent was certain. The trial involved three men who later became outstanding citizens. Richard Howell, accused arsonist, became governor of New Jersey in 1792. He was succeeded in 1801 by Joseph Bloomfield, counsel for the seven defendants. Sheriff Elmer was elected one of New Jersey's first two United States senators after the Constitution was adopted in 1789.

Governor Franklin convened the Assembly on January 11, 1775, at Perth Amboy. He spoke in careful language, warning that there were "two roads—one evidently leading to peace, happiness and a restoration of public tranquility—the other inevitably conducting you to anarchy, misery, and all the horrors of a Civil War." The governor asked the Assembly to draw up its list of grievances for him to submit to King George. Elias Boudinot, John DeHart, and William Livingston hastened to Perth Amboy to urge caution. The assemblymen decided to comply with Franklin's request.

The Assembly modeled its grievances after the "Declarations and Resolves" of the Continental Congress and approved the general recommendations of the assembled colonies. In addition, it protested that judges had not been made entirely dependent on the Assembly for their salaries or their terms in office, clearly having in mind Chief Justice Smyth, whose words in Newark had angered them. Franklin refused to forward the grievances to the King, as promised, so the Assembly sent its complaints directly, without the governor's sanction.

War Alert

There was no turning back. The militia went on the alert. Jemima Condict, a teen-age girl who lived on First Mountain west of Newark, told in her diary in the spring of 1775 of young Americans getting ready for war on the military greens of the area. She wrote:

> Monday, which was called Training Day, I rode with my dear father down to see them train, there being several companies met together. I thought it would be mournful sight to see, if they had been fighting in earnest, & how soon they will be

called forth to the field of war we can not tell, for by what we hear the quarrels are not likely to be made up without bloodshed. I have jest now heard say that all hopes of conciliation between Britain and her colonies are at an end, for both the King & his Parliament have announced our destruction; fleets and armies are preparing with utmost diligence for that purpose.

In other colonies, too, the tide of war was rising. Patrick Henry told the Virginia House of Burgesses in March, 1775, that "the next gale that sweeps from the North will bring to our ear the clash of resounding arms! Our brethren are already in the field." Within a month, on April 19, 1775, Minutemen at Lexington and Concord battled British regulars. When a horseman from Boston passed through Elizabeth, New Brunswick, Princeton, and Trenton on April 23 and 24 with news of Lexington and Concord, the "gale" roared over New Jersey. Newark leaders ordered the militia company to exercise every week.

New Jersey's own Liberty Bell is in the museum in the Cumberland courthouse in Bridgeton. It was tolled on July 4, 1776.

Morris County organized three hundred volunteers. A militia company marched by Franklin's mansion in Perth Amboy in May with "Colors, Drum and Fife."

The appalled governor reported to England that "ever since that unfortunate affair at Lexington the colonies have been in the utmost commotion." He tried in May to get the Assembly to accept an English offer that any colony willing to provide funds for its own government and defense would be relieved of duties and taxes except for the regulation of commerce. The Assembly replied, "We cannot suppose you to entertain a suspicion that the present house has the least design to desert the common cause, in which all America appears to be deeply interested and firmly united."

A New Jersey Provincial Congress that gathered in Trenton in May of 1775, to supersede the Assembly, included nine assemblymen among its eighty-seven delegates. The Congress announced a system of elections, the first regular elections since the days of the proprietors. Harsh military laws called for all physically fit men between sixteen and fifty to bear arms or be fined four shillings monthly. Anyone who refused would be "dealt with as they [a committee of safety] shall direct." It was said that regimentation was greater than any ever dreamed of by Parliament.

Franklin's Decision

When he met the Assembly in November, 1775, Franklin urged Jerseymen to remain loyal in the approaching storm. He recognized that it might be his last meeting with the Assembly, and he asked the delegates whether he should remain in New Jersey or flee. "It is high time that every man should know what he has to expect," the governor declared.

The legislators assured Franklin that the people of New Jersey meant him no harm. They sent a petition to King George beseeching him "to prevent the effusion of blood; and to express the great desire that this house hath to a restoration of peace and harmony with the parent state." New Jersey's delegates to the Continental Congress were asked to seek an early reconciliation between the colonies and the mother country. John Jay, George Wythe, and John Dickinson hastened from the Congress to plead with the New Jersey Assembly in Burlington. Dickinson told the assemblymen that Englishmen believed the colonies were "a rope of sand and would not fight." The Assembly wavered, then threw its support behind the Continental Congress—telling Franklin nevertheless that they knew of no sentiment for independence avowed by "men of consequence."

On January 8, 1776, Franklin was awakened by violent knocking on the door of his Perth Amboy home. The visitors so alarmed the ailing Mrs. Franklin that the governor said he was "not without apprehension of her dying with the fright." Soldiers waited while Colonel William Winds asked him if he would give his word of honor to stay in Perth Amboy. Franklin agreed, then violated his word by summoning the old Assembly to meet in Perth Amboy on June 20 in defiance of the Provincial Congress that had been elected in May. The Congress met in Burlington on June 10 to order Colonel Nathanial Heard of Middlesex to approach Franklin "with all the delicacy and tenderness which the nature of the business could possibly admit," and give him the choice of staying at Princeton, Bordentown, or at his own farm at Rancocas. Franklin refused parole, was arrested on June 17, and brought to Burlington under guard. He was sent to Connecticut, where he could be watched by Governor Jonathan Trumbull, known to be strongly against Great Britain. Franklin remained a loyalist to the end and went to England in 1782 to live out his years.

New Jersey Divided

Franklin's departure meant that war was imminent. New Jersey faced the action in a divided state. Newark and Burlington members of the Anglican Church stoutly favored remaining loyal to England, and there were enough loyalists in other places to form a New Jersey Battalion to fight against the Revolutionists. New Jersey's position be-

This room on the first floor of the Ford mansion in Morristown was used by George Washington as his office during the winter of 1779–1780, when he had his headquarters here. The Ford mansion was built in 1774 by Colonel Jacob Ford, an iron manufacturer and ardent patriot.

tween New York and Philadelphia made it certain that important battles soon must be fought here; many people preferred not to be either outspoken Tories or fiery Revolutionists.

New Jersey named five delegates to the Continental Congress on June 22, 1776, headed by the Reverend John Witherspoon, president of the College of New Jersey in Princeton. The other delegates were Richard Stockton of Princeton, a member of the first graduating class of the College of New Jersey, Abraham Clark of Essex County, John Hart of Hopewell, and Francis Hopkinson of Bordentown. They were instructed to join with other delegates at Philadelphia "in most vigorous measures for supporting the just rights and liberties of America." If necessary, they were to join "in declaring the United Colonies independent of Great Britain."

146

The State of New Jersey

Meanwhile, New Jersey's Provincial Congress prepared for the split. On June 24, Jacob Green of Morris County and his committee began writing a constitution for a proposed State of New Jersey. It was completed eight days later and became law on July 2 by the slimmest of margins. Of the sixty-five members of the Congress, thirty members did not vote at all. Of the thirty-five who voted, nine said nay. Thus only twenty-six members actually voted for the document, and thirty-nine either voted no or did not vote at all! As a final measure of caution the adopters agreed:

> If a reconciliation between Great Britain and these colonies should take place and the latter be taken again under protection and government of the crown of Great Britain, this charter shall be null and void.

That cautious clause was not unusual. Only New Hampshire and South Carolina preceded New Jersey in adopting state constitutions. Two days after New Jersey had accepted its constitution, its five delegates joined in adopting the Declaration of Independence in Philadelphia.

So the long journey from exploration to independence had been completed. New Jersey's seemingly reluctant movement to independence in the years just before the Declaration of Independence might be considered to have been based on fear of separating from the mother country. Yet, that revolutionary spirit had flared here almost from the time that Englishmen arrived.

There had been action against Governor Philip Carteret as early as 1670, featured by street riots in Elizabethtown. There had been ample bloodshed and open defiance of the King's representatives in most of East New Jersey by 1700. Then, in the 1740's, revolutionists openly defied the authority of the ruling class in at least a dozen communities. It was clear that the people, even when not led by a volatile Patrick Henry or a clever John Adams, believed firmly that neither England nor its officials had a right to declare what was best for people in a

new land thousands of miles away. These early New Jersey rebels knew that they had settled and had developed this country. They believed that it was theirs. They would fight for that belief.

By 1776, New Jersey was a state of many kinds of people. Descendants of the Swedes and the Finns still lived along the Delaware River. The Dutch were stronger than ever in the northeastern section of the state. The English colonists of the seventeenth century had been joined by Scots, Irish, French, and German settlers, who had come to add their national strengths to the New Jersey culture. New Jersey was indeed a genuine melting pot.

And war would come to this state with a vengeance. Washington would spend one third of the entire Revolution on New Jersey soil. His main army would be encamped in New Jersey for four of the first five winters of the war, and Washington himself would spend three of the first four winters of the war in the state. This middle colony would become the keystone of the Revolutionary War—the center of America, just as it had been in all its varied colonial days.

An artist's recreation of Trenton as it appeared during late colonial days. Although crude, this 1889 drawing was carefully made from old records and is a good representation of a New Jersey town at the beginning of the Revolution. Note General Washington waving to the people.

Bibliography

Atkinson, Joseph, *The History of Newark, New Jersey*. Newark: William B. Guild, 1878.

Bartlet, James B., and Jameson, J. F. (eds.), *Journal of Jasper Danckaerts, 1679–1680*. New York: Charles Scribner's Sons, 1913.

Bisbee, Henry H., *The New Jersey Business*. Burlington, New Jersey: Revell Press, 1963.

Craven, Wesley F., *New Jersey and the English Colonization of North America*. Princeton: D. Van Nostrand Co., Inc., 1964.

Cunningham, John T., *New Jersey: America's Main Road*. New York: Doubleday & Company, 1966.

———, *Newark*. Newark: The New Jersey Historical Society, 1966.

Dally, Joseph W., *Woodbridge and Vicinity*. Orig. pub. 1873. Reprinted Madison, New Jersey: The Hunterdon House, 1967.

Decker, Amelia S., *The Ancient Trail (The Old Mine Road)*. Trenton: Petty Printing Co., 1942.

Ellis, Franklin, *History of Monmouth County, N.J.* Philadelphia: R. T. Peck & Co., 1885.

Fiske, John, *The Dutch and Quaker Colonies in America*. Vols. VII, VIII of *The Historical Writings of John Fiske*. New York: Houghton, Mifflin and Company, 1902.

Gillies, John, *Memoirs of Rev. George Whitefield*. New Haven, Connecticut: Whitmore & Buckingham, 1834.

Hageman, John F., and Woodward, E. M., *History of Burlington and Mercer Counties*. Philadelphia: Everts & Peck, 1883.

Harrington, M. R., *The Indians of New Jersey: Dickon Among the Lenapes*. New Brunswick: Rutgers University Press, 1963.

Hine, C. G., *The Old Mine Road*. New Brunswick: Rutgers University Press, 1963.

Johnson, Amandus (trans.), *The Instruction for John Printz*. Philadelphia: Swedish Colonial Society, 1930.

——— *Swedish Settlements on the Delaware, 1638–1664*, Vols. I, II. Philadelphia: University of Pennsylvania Press, 1911.

Juet, Robert, *Juet's Journal*. Robert M. Lunny (ed.). Introd. by John T. Cunningham. Newark: The New Jersey Historical Society, 1959.

Kalm, Peter, *Travels in North America* (1750). Adolph B. Benson, ed. New York: Wilson-Erickson, Inc., 1937.

Kemmerer, Donald L., *Path to Freedom*. Princeton: Princeton University Press, 1940.

Kull, Irving S., (ed.). *New Jersey. A History*, Vols. I, II. New York: Lewis Historical Publishing Co., 1930.

Lane, Wheaton J., *From Indian Trail to Iron Horse*. Princeton: Princeton University Press, 1939.

Lee, Francis Bazley, *New Jersey As a Colony and State*, Vols. I and II. New York: The Publishing Society of New Jersey, 1902.

Leiby, Adrian C., *The Early Dutch and Swedish Settlers of New Jersey*. Princeton: D. Van Nostrand Co., Inc., 1964.

McCormick, Richard P., *New Jersey from Colony to State, 1609–1789*. Princeton: D. Van Nostrand Co., Inc., 1964.

Mellick, Andrew D., *The Story of an Old Farm, or, Life in New Jersey in the Eighteenth Century*. Somerville, New Jersey: The Unionist-Gazette, 1889. Reprinted in edited form as *Lesser Crossroads*, Hubert G. Schmidt (ed.). New Brunswick: Rutgers University Press, 1948.

New Jersey Historical Society, *New Jersey Archives, 1880–1893 1st Series*. Newark: The New Jersey Historical Society.

———— *Records of the Town of Newark, New Jersey*, from 1666. Newark: Reprinted 1864 by the New Jersey Historical Society. Reprinted again in 1966.

Peare, Catherine O., *John Woolman, Child of Light*. New York: Vanguard Press, 1954.

Pomfret, John E., *The New Jersey Proprietors and Their Lands*. Princeton: D. Van Nostrand Co., Inc., 1964.

————, *The Province of East New Jersey, 1609–1702*. Princeton: Princeton University Press, 1962.

————, *The Province of West New Jersey, 1609–1702*. Princeton: Princeton University Press, 1956.

Salem County Tercentenary Committee, *Fenwick's Colony*. Salem, New Jersey: Salem County Tercentenary Committee, 1964.

Sickler, Joseph S., *Old Houses of Salem County, New Jersey*. Salem, New Jersey: The Sunbeam Publishing Co., 1937.

————, *Tea Burning Town*. New York: Abelard Press, 1950.

Simpson, Hazel B. (ed.), *Under Four Flags*. Woodbury, New Jersey: Board of Chosen Freeholders of Gloucester, 1965.

Smith, Samuel, *The History of the Colony of Nova Caesaria, or New Jersey* (to the year 1721). Trenton: Wm. S. Sharp, 1877. (Original published in 1765.)

Stewart, Frank H., *Major John Fenwick*. Salem, New Jersey: Salem County Historical Society, 1964.

Tanner, Edwin P., *The Province of New Jersey, 1664–1738*. New York: Columbia University Press, 1908.

Thayer, Theodore, *As We Were, The Story of Old Elizabeth*. Newark: The New Jersey Historical Society, 1964.

Weiss, Harry B., *Life in Early New Jersey*. Princeton: D. Van Nostrand Co., Inc., 1964.

Weslager, C. A., *Dutch Explorers, Traders and Settlers in the Delaware Valley, 1609–1664*. Philadelphia: University of Pennsylvania Press, 1964.

———, *The English on the Delaware, 1610–1682*. New Brunswick: Rutgers University Press, 1967.

Whitehead, William A., *Contributions to the Early History of Perth Amboy and Vicinity*. New York: D. Appleton & Company, 1856.

Important Dates

1498	Cabots explore off present-day New Jersey coast.
1524	Giovanni da Verrazano explores lower Hudson River.
1609	Henry Hudson explores Delaware Bay, the Jersey coast, New York Bay, and Sandy Hook Bay.
1623	Dutch establish Fort Nassau on Delaware River.
1638	New Sweden begins beside lower Delaware River.
1650	Dutch adventurers find copper in Kittatinny Mountains.
1655	New Sweden captured by Dutch under Peter Stuyvesant.
1660	Bergen (now part of Jersey City) founded as first town in New Jersey.
1664	England conquers New Amsterdam; Duke of York deeds land to Berkeley and Carteret and gives New Jersey its name.
1665	Philip Carteret becomes first governor. Middletown and Shrewsbury founded.
1666	Newark, Piscataway, and Woodbridge founded.
1668	First New Jersey Legislature convenes.
1670	First troubles over land ownership.
1674	First ironworks established at Shrewsbury.
1675	John Fenwick settles Salem.
1676	William Penn gets official agreement for establishment of West New Jersey.
1681	Burlington named West New Jersey capital.
1686	Capital of East New Jersey set in Perth Amboy.
1700	First northern New Jersey ironworks opened at Hanover.
1700–1701	"The Revolution" rocks New Jersey.
1702	East and West New Jersey combined into a single province by Queen Anne.
1737	Population of New Jersey 47,402.
1738	First governor of New Jersey as a province separate from New York is Lewis Morris.

1739	New Jersey's first glassworks established in Salem County.
1745	Population 61,383.
1745–1750	Series of wild riots shake many parts of New Jersey, particularly Essex County.
1746	College of New Jersey (now Princeton University) founded in Elizabeth; moved to Newark in 1747 and then to Princeton in 1756.
1758	America's first Indian reservation set up at Indian Mills.
1763	William Franklin starts rule as last royal governor.
1766	Queen's College (now Rutgers, the State University) opened in New Brunswick.
1774	First Provincial Congress meets in New Brunswick; declares loyalty to England but protests taxes. New Jersey's own "tea party" at Greenwich in December.
1776	Governor Franklin is arrested; Provincial Congress adopts State Constitution on July 2.

Historic Sites

BELCHER MANSION, 1046 East Jersey Street, Elizabeth, built before 1722. Jonathan Belcher, royal governor of New Jersey, lived here from 1751 until his death in 1757. Recently restored.

BOXWOOD HALL, also known as the Boudinot House, Elizabeth, erected *c.* 1750 and named for boxwood that surrounded it. Many important people, including George Washington, met here as guests of Elias Boudinot. Now a state-owned house.

DEY MANSION, Totowa Road, Mountain View, built in 1740 for Col. Theunis Dey, wealthy Dutch landowner. Washington had his headquarters here during summer and fall of 1780.

ESSEX COUNTY COURTHOUSE, Springfield Avenue, Newark, is distinguished by two large murals of colonial days. One, by Howard Pyle, shows the landing of Philip Carteret at Elizabethtown in 1665; the other, by C. Y. Turner, shows the landing of Robert Treat and his followers at Newark in 1666.

ALEXANDER GRANT HOUSE, 83 Market Street, Salem, built 1721. Now home of Salem County Historical Society.

GREENWICH, southwest of Bridgeton, site of New Jersey's own "tea party" on December 22, 1774. Sleepy little town clustered around Tea Burners Monument has changed very little.

HACKENSACK GREEN, south end Main Street, set aside by Hackensack's first settlers. Original court house built here in 1732, burned during Revolution. The *Church on the Green* (First Dutch Reformed) has portion that dates to 1696.

WILLIAM HANCOCK HOUSE, Salem County. Built 1734, this patterned brick house has date and initials of builders in the gable. On March 20, 1778, colonial troops were massacred in the attic. Behind the house is a cedar-plank log cabin built by Swedish settlers more than two hundred years ago.

INDIAN KING INN, 233 Kings Highway East, Haddonfield, is a state-owned historic house built in 1751. New Jersey's first state legislature met here in 1777. Dolly Madison was a regular visitor.

LAWRENCEVILLE, Route 206, S.W. of Princeton. The red brick PRESBY-TERIAN CHURCH was built in 1716.

MARLPIT HALL, King's Highway, Middletown, a wide-shingled Dutch-type building erected *c.* 1684. Maintained as a museum.

MILITARY PARK and WASHINGTON PARK, Newark, as well as BROAD STREET, where they touch, date to the original town laid out in 1667. *Trinity Episcopal Church* on Military Park dates to 1743. Also on Broad Street, about a quarter mile north of Washing-ton Park, is the *John Plume House,* built in 1710, the oldest house in Newark.

NASSAU HALL on Princeton University campus. Finished in 1756, when the College of New Jersey moved there from Newark. A center of fighting during Revolution. Adjacent is the *Dean's House,* built in 1756 and occupied by all Princeton presidents to 1879.

NATIONAL HISTORICAL PARK, Morristown, includes the *Jacob Ford Mansion,* Revolutionary war museum, built in 1774, where Wash-ington lived in the winter of 1779, and *Jockey Hollow,* where his troops were quartered. The *Tempe Wick House* in Jockey Hollow was built in 1746 as a characteristic "New England" type farm-house.

OLD BARRACKS, South Willow Street, Trenton, the only barracks left from five built in New Jersey, 1758-1759, to house English troops during the French and Indian War. Used by Hessians during Revolution before the Battle of Trenton.

OLD CEDAR MEETING HOUSE, Route 9, Seaville, Cape May County. Little wooden Quaker building erected in 1716.

OLD ST. MARY'S CHURCH, West Broad Street, Burlington. Built 1703, is oldest Episcopal Church building in New Jersey.

OLD TENNENT CHURCH, on edge of fields where the Battle of Mon-mouth was fought in 1778. The shingled church, built in 1751, is a fine example of a colonial church, inside and out.

POMONA HALL, also known as Charles S. Boyer Memorial Hall, Camden. Built 1726. Headquarters of Camden County Historical Society. Patterned brick house.

RINGWOOD, off Route 511 near New York border, has little left of the days when "Baron" Hasenclever developed a great iron empire. However, this state-owned site has a handsome manor house and grounds that tell the story of Ringwood's past glories.

SALEM OAK, in Friends Burial Grounds on West Broadway, Salem, estimated to be more than five hundred years old. John Fenwick is said to have bargained with Indians here in 1675. Original Quaker settlers lie in its shade.

SANDY HOOK. Isolation as a military base has preserved the Hook much as it was three hundred years ago. America's oldest continuously lit lighthouse, built in 1763, is still operating. The country's oldest holly trees are in the area, as they were when colonists arrived. The lower part of the Hook is a public bathing beach.

SHREWSBURY, Route 35, Monmouth County. On northwest corner Broad St. & Sycamore Ave. is the *Allen House*, built 1667. On opposite corner is the handsome *Christ Episcopal Church*, built 1769. Its Georgian colonial tower is topped by a weather vane in the shape of an iron British crown.

VON STEUBEN HOUSE, Main Street, New Bridge (or River Edge). Built *c.* 1700 by the Ackerman family. This house later was owned by John Zabriski. It was offered after the Revolution to Baron von Steuben for his services to the American cause. He never occupied it.

SURVEYOR GENERAL'S OFFICE, City Hall Square, Perth Amboy, is home of the East New Jersey proprietors whose role in New Jersey history dates back nearly three hundred years.

TRENT HOUSE, on Warren Street, Trenton, in east part of city. Built *c.* 1719 by William Trent, the brick house has been called "one of the finest Queen Anne period houses in America."

WEST NEW JERSEY PROPRIETORS Office, Broad Street, Burlington, home of Quaker proprietors, whose corporate beginnings date back to 1676.

Index